Feedback for

The New Directors Handbook

This could become the definitive guide; a must read for new boards, new listings, small and medium companies. I shall certainly use it – of that there is no doubt – for my companies.

– Nigel Payne, Chairman of AIM listed company

We do need to reassure/inspire individuals to become NED's and this book does just that. A reliable read that de-mystifies the role.

- Jerry Blackett, Chief Executive, Birmingham Chamber of Commerce

A superb exposition of all the facts people should take into account for a first time appointment. This book is also a very good aide memoir for those already in Office as a reminder of their responsibilities.

- Tony Collinson, Principal, Lionel James Accountants

This book is an invaluable tool for new directors and for anyone in management or aspiring to be so. It is a concentrated 'one stop shop' of theories, tools and frameworks that will help any individual or organisation. A great aide memoire written in such a way that cuts out unnecessary text and has clear explanations and diagrams.

- Paula Fowler, Managing Partner, Fisher Jones Greenwood, solicitors

This is a practical, no no-nonsense guide for both new directors and for those who have been directors for some time. It explains both the responsibilities of directors and how these responsibilities can be approached. The book is well laid out and easy to follow. A particularly useful section is the transition from manager to director - which many people find particularly difficult.

- Ann Bentley, Chairman of the Global Boar, Rider Levett Bucknall

The AIM Directors Handbook

Richard Winfield

Brefi Press
www.brefipress.com

Cover design and diagrams by Chris Walker, Expressive Design.

First published in 2016 by Brefi Press

ISBN 978-0-948537-17-2

www.brefipress.com

Books by Richard Winfield

The New Directors Handbook

Reflections of a Corporate Coach

Stories from a Corporate Coach

Lessons from a Corporate Coach – Coaching

Lessons from a Corporate Coach – Business

www.brefipress.com

About the author

Richard Winfield is the founder and principal consultant of Brefi Group and head of the Director Development Centre.

He is a strategy consultant, facilitator and scenario planner who provides transition coaching to directors, boards and partnerships and helps them develop strategy and build teams. His instinctive creativity is in establishing objectives, defining strategies and assessing priorities.

Richard has a natural talent for collecting, integrating and simplifying ideas and then communicating them to others. He is the guy to call when you need to bring structure and clarity to your thinking. He helps you identify core issues and make the complex simple, holding the space for you to create your own solutions.

Richard has thirty years experience as a management development consultant, including helping the first magistrates' courts service and the first local authority in Wales to earn Investor in People status and a two and a half year management development contract for National Power.

Throughout his career he has been committed to community building and getting systems change to make things better. He is passionate about setting people free to achieve their untapped potential and is continually analysing, simplifying and improving.

He is highly qualified with a rich and varied career covering start-ups, privatisations and acquisitions with small, large and international organisations, public, private and third sector in the UK, Europe, USA, Middle East, Asia and Africa. A chameleon, he easily absorbs and relates to different cultures, whether they be organisational or geographical.

In the late 1960s Richard gained an honours degree in civil engineering and a master's degree in highways and transportation, followed by a ten year career as a transportation planner, for which he won an international silver medal.

Since 1990 he has focused on management development and, more recently, on director development and corporate governance.

In 2001 he launched the *CorporateCoach* newsletter, which has had more than 20,000 readers.

He launched the Director Development Centre in 2009, combining his interests in strategy and structure with the increasing demand for improved standards of corporate governance.

In 2010 he launched the School of Executive Coaching to design, license and deliver coach training in Africa, Asia and the Middle East, and in 2011 registered Invisible Coaching© as a proprietary coaching system for individuals.

Richard has extensive consulting and training experience in the UK, North America, Europe, South and West Africa, Baltic states, Arabian Gulf, India and South East Asia. For three years he was responsible for developing the directors and senior managers of an international engineering group, reporting direct to the chief executive. He is co-founder of the Landor Publishing Group and served two terms as a director of Birmingham Forward.

Richard is a Master Practitioner of both NLP and Wealth Dynamics, and has been trained in leadership at the Disney Institute in Florida. He is the creator of 'Invisible Coaching® - the art of natural coaching', is a past governor of the International Association of Coaching and has published five books on coaching.

He is addicted to learning and personal development; he has studied with thought leaders in North America, Europe and Asia, and reads widely.

As well as reading, he enjoys vegetable gardening, landscape gardening, pond building and cycling. He has been a farmer, worked as a cowboy and is now an established author.

Contents

Preface

If you are ready to grow your company and need to raise external finance, you might be considering the Alternative Investment Market (AIM).

AIM was established to meet the needs of small and medium-sized companies seeking to develop their business by raising external finance from capital markets within a simplified regulatory environment.

Before deciding whether to embark on an AIM flotation you should consider carefully the issues involved in joining a public market. Such a decision brings responsibilities as well as benefits. People at every level of the business, from board members to employees, must be ready to accept the disciplines inherent in having shares traded publicly, and in having outside shareholders whose interests must be taken into account.

Flotation on a public market will inevitably lead to closer scrutiny of the company, its performance and its directors. In general, the board must be prepared for greater transparency, both in terms of the company's finances and business strategy and in having to make prompt announcements about new developments, whether positive or negative.

This book provides an introduction to AIM and the process of application to help you decide whether it is right for you. As a director of an AIM company your actions and decisions become more transparent and your responsibilities to shareholders more demanding.

Whether you are already a director of an AIM listed company, a private company considering a flotation, or even a company with a full listing on the London Stock Exchange, a thorough understanding of effective behaviours and good practice will enable you to achieve the level of performance required, and make a positive contribution to the companies you serve.

Where regulation and litigation are concerned, ignorance is not an excuse. The AIM Directors Handbook covers directors' roles and responsibilities, board processes, corporate governance and strategy to support you in achieving the enhanced levels of performance and compliance that will be expected of you as a director of a quoted public company.

As its title suggests, it is a handbook. Read it through and it will provide you with a comprehensive foundation for your career as a director. Then use it as a reference and return to it when you need to.

As a director, you serve at the top of a company where you have the greatest leverage and opportunity to contribute and make a difference. I wish you well in that endeavour.

Richard Winfield
February 2016

Richard Winfield

The AIM Directors Handbook

1. Could AIM be the right choice for you?

Are you ready to grow your company? Do you need to strengthen your board, upgrade your processes, adopt formal corporate governance practice? Do you need to raise external finance? If so, the Alternative Investment Market (AIM) could be just the route for you.

As a company grows it needs to evolve. It needs to grow its management team beyond its original founders, introduce good practices and processes and start thinking in terms of good corporate governance. There may come a time when funds available from your bank and from private sources are no longer sufficient to sustain your capital requirements.

If you have already tapped angels and venture capitalists, and if key staff have been rewarded with shares or options, they will want to be able to value and, at some stage, realise their investment.

The traditional route to a flotation on a national stock exchange is extremely expensive and demanding, and you might not yet be eligible anyway.

However, there is an alternative.

AIM was established in June 1995 as part of the London Stock Exchange to meet the needs of small and medium-sized companies by bridging the gap for growing companies as they seek to develop their business through the use of external finance from capital markets. Its regulatory structure allows growing companies to cost effectively raise capital at admission and throughout their life on AIM.

Its balanced regulatory environment suits the needs of growing companies, with all the benefits of a public stock market quotation; and it is available worldwide.

More than 3,500 companies in more than 100 countries have joined AIM in its 20 year history, having raised over £90 billion through new and further issues to support their growth and development, making AIM the most successful public equity market for growth companies anywhere in the world.

Central to the development and success of AIM have been:

- A network of advisors and liquidity providers who understand the needs of growing companies and are able to support them throughout their journey as a public company;
- A regulatory approach that recognises the needs and capacities of growth companies, and
- A diverse and highly knowledgeable investor base that can effectively provide capital to support growing companies.

AIM companies have access to a range of institutional investors, a vibrant cohort of retail investors and, thanks to London's unique status, an unparalleled pool of international capital, including traditional institutions, hedge funds, retail investors through private client brokers, family offices and high net worth individuals.

While for most companies, admission to AIM forms part of a fundraising exercise, there are other good reasons for a company to float on AIM. These include expanding your ability to acquire other businesses by issuing quoted shares, establishing a value for the business and enhancing the effectiveness of any employee incentive programmes or share option schemes.

Here are some of the reasons why companies have chosen AIM:

- Fewer barriers to entry and ongoing compliance requirements are less burdensome;
- No minimum market capitalisation needed;
- Suitable for companies seeking growth and new capital which have little or no trading record;
- No need for prior shareholder approval for transactions unless the ratios exceed 100% in any of the class tests (i.e. reverse takeover or a fundamental disposal); this compares with the 25% threshold for an official list company;
- AIM shares are treated as "unquoted" for tax purposes and, accordingly, certain tax incentives are offered to investors and companies which meet the relevant qualifying conditions including, in the case of individuals, enterprise investment relief and reinvestment relief; and
- No requirement to have a minimum number of shares in public hands. However, there should be sufficient "free float" liquidity in a company's shares.

Companies joining AIM gain many of the advantages experienced by companies with a full listing on the Main Market, including access to a unique, globally-respected market and a deep pool of capital; enhanced profile and heightened interest in your company; and increased status and credibility.

The flexibility offered by AIM is confirmed by a comparison with the requirements involved in the listing on the London Stock Exchange's Main Market.

AIM	Main Market
No prescribed level of shares to be in public hands	Minimum 25% shares in public hands
No trading record requirement	Normally three-year trading record is required
No prior shareholder approval for most transactions*	Prior shareholder approval required for substantial acquisitions and disposals
Admission documents not pre-vetted by the Exchange nor by the UK Listing Authority (UKLA) in most circumstances.	Pre-vetting of prospectus by the UKLA
Nominated adviser required at all times	Sponsors needed for certain transactions
No minimum market capitalisation	Minimum market capitalisation

* not applicable to reverse takeovers or disposals resulting in a fundamental change of business

Joining a public market

Before deciding whether to embark on an AIM flotation you should consider carefully the issues involved in joining a public market. Such a decision brings responsibilities as well as benefits. People at every level of the business, from board members to employees, must be ready to accept the disciplines inherent in having shares traded publicly, and in having outside shareholders whose interests must be taken into account.

In particular, you should be aware that flotation on a public market brings with it an exposure to the uncertainty of market conditions. The company's share price may be affected by a number of factors beyond its control, including market sentiment, economic conditions or developments in the same sector.

A further change to bear in mind is that flotation will inevitably lead to closer scrutiny of the company, its performance and its directors. In general, the board must be prepared for greater transparency, both in terms of the company's finances and business strategy and in having to make prompt announcements about new developments, whether positive or negative.

A strong support community

AIM is supported by a highly experienced and knowledgeable community of advisors and liquidity providers, who will be able to support you throughout your company's lifetime on AIM, from the initial admission process and thereafter on its journey as a public company.

The IPO process consists of three main phases: due diligence, documentation and marketing. The process could be undertaken within three to four months depending on the availability of the information required for the due diligence phase and the availability and access to management and its supporting team throughout the process.

However, in practice, the interval between the decision of the board to seek admission to AIM and admission itself is often a great deal longer than this, since thought must be given to matters such as a group structure, corporate governance and financial controls and the putting in place of appropriate share-based incentive schemes for the employees of the company.

The Nomad

When the London Stock Exchange created AIM in 1995, it sought to establish a sensible and practical method of regulation that would be appropriate for the younger, smaller companies that it wanted to attract. Realising that many smaller companies would not have a management team with experience of running public companies, the exchange chose to devolve the responsibility for ongoing regulation of its aim companies. It achieved this by creating a new type of financial advisor, the Nomad, with authority and responsibility to decide whether a company is suitable for admission to AIM and to provide it with ongoing advice.

Nomads are authorised by the London Stock Exchange based on their experience of dealing with publicly quoted companies; they include accounting firms, investment banks, corporate finance firms and stockbrokers.

Such is the importance of the role of the Nomad that AIM companies are required to retain one at all times. Without a Nomad, a company is effectively unregulated and under the AIM rules it will have its shares suspended and eventually will have its admission to AIM cancelled. This is a serious issue as cancellation will mean that the shares can no longer be traded by shareholders.

The typical cost for appointing a Nomad to advise on admission to AIM is usually calculated as a percentage of any new money raised, typically between three and five per cent of the value of the issue, depending on the nature of the obligations assumed by the Nomad (and inclusive of sub-underwriting commissions). Additionally a corporate finance fee is generally charged.

So, if you wish to join AIM you will need to appoint a nominated adviser (Nomad) to be your key adviser during the admission process and while it is quoted on AIM.

Choose your Nomad carefully; they will be your professional adviser and friend for the long term, guiding you through the process and acting as your regulator. Your Nomad will decide whether your company is suitable for admission to AIM and be responsible for ongoing regulation of your behaviour once admitted, as well as providing you with advice on your obligations under the AIM Rules.

The Nomad has three principal tasks:

- determining if the company is appropriate for admission;
- managing the flotation process; and, after flotation,
- advising the AIM company in respect of its compliance with the AIM Rules and general corporate governance.

As an AIM company you will have an obligation to seek advice from your Nomad regarding compliance with the AIM Rules and to take that advice into account. The issues on which you must take advice include a range of scenarios from changes to the board, changes in exposure expectations for trading, directors wishing to buy or sell shares, and corporate activity, whether buying or selling companies or assets.

In addition to the Nomad, you will need to appoint a number of other advisors to support you throughout the admission process. These include a broker, reporting accountant, law firm, market maker, public relations firm, and registrar. Note that this list does not include management consultants or any specific service to support you in improving corporate governance or the performance of the board.

The team of advisors that you choose to appoint will be integral in supporting you throughout the flotation process and once admitted to AIM. It is important to select firms that have appropriate sector and market experience and are committed to working with you after admission; it is vital to have personal chemistry with your advisors, since you will be working very closely together.

Reporting Accountants

The reporting accountants may or may not be the same firm as the company's existing auditors but their role is somewhat different. Their principal role is to conduct an in-depth review of the company's financial position, reporting systems and working capital requirements, and to report to the Nomad on any areas of concern, primarily by way of a long form report which will also include a detailed review of the business and assets of the company.

The reporting accountant's financial expertise, as well as its experience with the rigours and peculiarities of the flotation process will help smooth the directors' progression through the process as they can quickly identify and assist in the resolution of issues that might otherwise hold up an AIM admission.

Corporate lawyer

There is a need for at least two firms of lawyers on an AIM flotation and in any secondary issue by an AIM company – lawyers to act for the company and lawyers to act to the nominated advisor or Nomad and the broker.

The company's lawyers play a central role in the flotation process, advising on the structuring of the company and its subsidiaries, on the documentation involved and on the responsibilities of the directors in relation to the flotation and any associated fundraising.

They will advise on the legal aspects of preparing the company for admission to AIM and will undertake a legal review required by the Nomad for the purposes of satisfying itself of the appropriateness of the company for admission to AIM.

The lawyers for the Nomad and the broker are responsible for reviewing the admission document and supporting documentation, as well as any other investment communications proposed to be issued by the Nomad and the broker.

As legal and financial due diligence processes run in parallel, they impose substantial demands on management's time and you will need to make provision for management to be able to commit the necessary time to the process, whilst still running the business.

Nominated broker

An AIM company must retain the services of a nominated broker at all times. The broker is responsible for raising funds for the business and for developing and maintaining good relations with the investment community. After the flotation the broker will work with you to create and maintain a market in the company's shares.

Because of the size of most AIM companies and the cost associated with a full public offering, a 'placing' is the most common method of issue on AIM. In a placing, the broker sells the company's securities to professional investors using an admission document. Larger companies seeking to raise large amounts of capital may consider a public offer where the securities are issued to the public via a prospectus.

While the roles of a Nomad and a broker are distinct, they are commonly performed by the same organisation. However, it is important to understand that the roles are completely different and separate. The Nomad's client is the company and its dealings with the company are private. The broker's clients are its institutional investors and it must not be privy to the confidential communications between the Nomad and the AIM company.

Where one the firm plays both roles, there must be a clear separation of responsibilities and a 'Chinese wall' must be established between the two parts of that firm.

Financial PR consultants

PR advisers form an essential part of the advisory team and should have a broad and deep knowledge of the regulatory requirements that any company seeking to join AIM must meet. Their role is to generate positive press interest and publicity and to monitor the content and wording of any public statements.

Besides designing and implementing a communications strategy for the IPO process itself, the PR firm should also act as the company's eyes and ears within the media and investment community. The strength of its relationships with the financial media and analyst community will enable it to judge market sentiment towards the company and its proposed offering, as well as to monitor sentiment towards the sector in general.

Implications for the directors

For quoted companies, it is essential to ensure that the interests of all shareholders are protected and that the interests of management and shareholders are closely aligned. Keeping investors informed about the company will become crucial if the business is to reap the maximum potential benefit from being publicly quoted.

The AIM Rules will require you to have in place sufficient procedures, resources and controls to enable compliance. This is more than just producing management accounts to show whether trading is in line with budget, but extends to the board understanding the rules, identifying when directors or key employees want to trade the shares, and knowing when there are close periods, amongst other matters.

Many private companies lack an appropriate level of corporate governance at the outset. Whilst AIM companies are not required to comply with the full UK Corporate Governance Code, the Quoted Companies Alliance has developed a set of 12 essential principles which represent good practice for small and mid-sized quoted companies and the Nomad would expect these to be followed:

Delivering growth in long-term shareholder value:

1. Setting out the vision and strategy
2. Managing and communicating risk and implementing internal control
3. Articulating strategy through corporate communication and investor relations
4. Meeting the needs and objectives of your shareholders
5. Meeting shareholder and social responsibilities
6. Using cost-effective and value-added arrangements

Maintaining a flexible, efficient and effective management framework within an entrepreneurial environment:

7. Developing structures and processes
8. Being responsible and accountable
9. Having balance on the board
10. Having appropriate skills and capabilities on the board
11. Evaluating board performance and development
12. Providing information and support

Corporate governance is discussed in more detail later in this book.

Recruiting new directors

In most cases, companies seeking an IPO will need to recruit new directors to their board; you will need at least two independent non-executive directors on the board to represent the interests of outside shareholders.

If the company has been dependent on the leadership of a few key individuals, you may also need to demonstrate that there is a management development and succession plan in place to enable sustainable growth, and to undertake a review of board processes against corporate governance standards. For example, it is desirable to separate the roles of chairman and chief executive.

The importance of the board cannot be underestimated in setting the tone for compliance and also ensuring adherence to the rules. Nomads are responsible for ensuring that the company remains suitable for trading on AIM and will, therefore, take a lot of care to understand the background of anyone appointed to the board.

Potential appointees will be asked to complete a questionnaire by the Nomad, and may well also have their CV vetted by an independent third-party.

If non-executive directors become involved with the company early enough in the IPO process they can have a significant input into the IPO preparation. When making your selection, it's important to recognise that the fit between the proposed directors, the executive team and the original shareholders is as important as the new directors' skills and experience.

If the founder directors are integral members of the board, they must consider any additional obligations that may be imposed upon them as a result of taking the company to AIM. They may also wish to take financial advice to ensure that their personal tax planning is not jeopardised by the admission process.

Restructuring

It is not unusual for some corporate restructuring to take place prior to admission. If the company seeking admission is a private limited company, it may well have to re-register as a public limited company (plc). Alternatively, it may be preferable to create a group structure, or reorganise an existing group so that the holding company of the group is a public limited company.

In the UK only public limited companies may offer their shares to the public; the nominal value of a UK plc's share capital must not be less than £50,000 and not less than 25% of the nominal value of the shares allotted and the whole of any premium must be paid up.

All of the shares of a particular class must be admitted to trading on AIM.

Shareholdings

Where individual directors have a substantial shareholding in the company, for example 30% of the voting shares, then they will typically be expected to enter into a relationship agreement with the company and the Nomad to ensure that all future transactions between the company and that shareholder are on arm's-length terms and on a normal commercial basis and that the company is capable of carrying on its business independently of them at all times.

This may represent a significant shift in historic practice to the company and should be considered early on.

As an AIM company, it is important to ensure that there is sufficient liquidity in the company's shares. This means a sufficient level of trading to facilitate the buying and selling of shares. Liquidity is linked, amongst other things, to the number of shareholders, the market capitalisation and the number of shares in the company.

However, if your company has not been independent and earning revenue for at least two years, you must ensure that all "related parties" agree not to dispose of any interest in its shares for one year from the date of admission. This includes directors of the company or any of its subsidiary, sister or parent undertakings, shareholders holding directly or indirectly 10% or more of any class of shares to be admitted to AIM, and employees of the company, its subsidiary or parent undertakings who, together with their family, have a holding interest directly or indirectly in 0.5% or more of a class of shares to be committed to AIM.

Guarantees

As well as having responsibility for the contents of the admission document, all the directors will have ongoing obligations as directors of an AIM company. The company's lawyers will provide you with a memorandum setting these out.

If a company issues shares as part of the flotation, a prospectus will be required. You should be aware that directors will be expected to give warranties to the Nomad relating to the prospectus/ admission documents and the company's business generally.

Should the prospectus be shown to be misleading, those responsible for it, including staff and professional advisers, could be liable to pay compensation to any shareholders who suffer loss as a result.

Management and key employees

The strength of the management team will be a critical consideration for institutional investors in deciding whether to invest in your company.

You should review your current team in terms of:

- Quality of management team
- Experience of management team
- Personal chemistry within the team
- Remuneration

In order to guarantee continuity through and beyond the flotation, it might be worth considering introducing share-based compensation plans to incentivise management and key employees. Whether such plans are already in existence or may be put in place after the flotation, they will need to be carefully considered to ensure that there are no adverse tax and/or accounting consequences to individuals or to the company.

If proper planning is not undertaken early on, this can potentially derail the flotation process at a later stage.

Your role, responsibilities and behaviours as a director

As a director, you serve at the top of a company where you have the greatest leverage and opportunity to contribute and make a difference.

As a director of an AIM company your actions and decisions will become more transparent and your responsibilities to shareholders more demanding. The remainder of this book covers the roles, responsibilities and practices of directors and boards.

As its title suggests, it is a handbook. Read it through and it will provide you with a comprehensive foundation for your career as a director. Then use it as a reference and return to it when you need to.

Where regulation and litigation are concerned, ignorance is not an excuse. This book will introduce you to the roles, responsibilities and risks you should be aware of as a director as well as providing you with some tools to help you in your career.

However, it cannot tell you everything, it cannot deal with changing business environments and legislation, and it cannot apply perfectly in every jurisdiction.

But if you know what you are looking for you can find out most of what you need to keep up to date by researching the Internet, and, of course, you should make good use of your Nomad or be prepared to consult one of the other external advisors provided by the AIM requirements.

Whether you are already a director of an AIM listed company, a private company, or even a company with a full listing on the London Stock Exchange, a thorough understanding of effective behaviours and good practice will enable you to become more confident, more effective, more quickly, with the knowledge and tools to become an excellent director, making a positive contribution to the companies you serve and being less exposed to developments and surprises that can put you at risk.

Further sources

The London Stock Exchange publishes useful brochures and documents, including guides to AIM, rules and regulations, and lists of Nomads and advisers.

http://www.londonstockexchange.com/companies-and-advisors/aim/aim/aim.htm

2. Company Directors and the Functions of a Board

What is a company?

A company is a legal entity. In law it is a 'person' and acts and takes decisions independently in its own right.

It is formed when two or more people come together for a common business goal. It has what is termed a 'separate legal personality' meaning it is treated as an entity separate from its shareholders. Consequently, the liabilities of a company cannot be extended to its shareholders. The liability of shareholders is limited to the amount unpaid on their shares.

As a legal entity, a company has, subject to the Companies Act of the jurisdiction where it is formed and to such limitations as are inherent in its corporate nature, the capacity, rights, powers and privileges of an individual. This entails that a company can own property, sue and be sued and enjoys perpetual succession, among others. However, a company is a lot more than a fiscal entity. It is a living thing.

The limited company structure has a number of advantages:

- It enables capital to be raised whilst limiting the financial exposure of the shareholders
- It provides for simple transferability of ownership through the buying and selling of shares
- It gives continuity to the business beyond the life of the original founders. In a sense companies, unlike the human beings who create them, have perpetuity; although if a company is unsuccessful, it will still die.

Since a company, unlike a human being, is an artificial person, it can only act through an agent, namely, a board of directors.

Companies exist in different forms:

- Public limited company (plc)
- Private limited company
- Subsidiary or group company
- Family business

- Company limited by guarantee
- Company formed by statute or government charter

However, the same rules apply in each. The company is a legal entity and the directors are appointed by the shareholders as stewards of its good health. Although they represent the shareholders, they do not work for them; they work for the company and sometimes there could be a conflict between the shareholders' interests and the company's interest.

A public company (plc) is one that is registered and describes itself as such. In the UK, only a plc may invite members of the public to subscribe for its shares.

A private company may not offer its shares to the general public. Usually the number of share-owners is restricted to a relatively small group of people closely connected with the company.

While management of day-to-day affairs is the responsibility of the management team, the board of directors is responsible for monitoring and overseeing management action.

The board are directly accountable to the shareholders and each year the company will hold an annual general meeting (AGM) at which the directors must provide a report to shareholders on the performance of the company, what its future plans and strategies are, and also submit themselves for re-election to the board.

The objects of the company are defined in the Memorandum of Association and regulations are laid out in the Articles of Association.

What is a director?

"A company director is one of the group of managers at the highest level in a company who control it and are in charge of making decisions about how it is run."

Cambridge Business English Dictionary

"A company director is an appointed or elected member of the board of directors of a company who, with other directors, has the responsibility for determining and implementing the company's policy."

BusinessDictionary.com

In the context of this text, a director is an individual who has been appointed to the board of directors of a limited company and who incurs the full stewardship and legal responsibilities of that position.

Directorship is a hands-off approach to value creation that complements c-suite leadership. Focused on value, directorship describes what boards do to create strong, resilient and enduring organisations.

Directors hold a position of trust on behalf of the shareholders and direct the company's operations on their behalf. The extent of the directors' authority depends on the company's Articles of Association.

The board of directors' key purpose is to ensure the company's prosperity by collectively directing the company's affairs, whilst meeting the appropriate interests of its shareholders and stakeholders. In addition to business and financial issues, boards of directors must deal with challenges and issues relating to corporate governance, corporate social responsibility and corporate ethics.

To ensure good governance, the board of directors should establish strategic objectives, policies and procedures that will guide and direct the organisation's activities; it should provide the necessary resources and a mechanism for monitoring the management's performance.

It is important that board meetings are held periodically so that directors can discharge their responsibility to control the company's overall situation, strategy and policy, and to monitor the exercise of any delegated authority; and so that individual directors can report on their particular areas of responsibility.

Every meeting must have a chairman, whose duties are to ensure that the meeting is conducted in such a way that the business for which it was convened is properly attended to, and that all those entitled to may express their views and that the decisions taken by the meeting adequately reflect the views of the meeting as a whole. The chairman will also very often decide upon the agenda and might sign off the minutes on his or her own authority.

Individual directors have only those powers that have been given to them by the board. Such authority need not be specific or in writing and may be inferred from past practice. However, the board as a whole remains responsible for actions carried out by its authority and it should therefore ensure that executive authority is only granted to appropriate persons and that adequate reporting systems enable it to maintain overall control.

The chairman of the board is often seen as the spokesperson for the board and the company.

Why become a director?

Why would anybody want to become a director?

Directorships bring risk, responsibility and no privileges!

Companies need directors to constitute a board and to direct their operations.

But why would anyone choose to become a director?

Let's get one thing straight first. Becoming a director has no relation with owning shares; you can be a director without owning shares, and you can own shares without becoming a director.

There are three elements in a company:

- the company itself
- the shareholders
- the directors

And these are entirely independent.

In addition there is a whole range of stakeholders to consider.

Health risk!

The next thing for you to understand is that limited liability applies to the company; it does not apply to the directors. It is important that you understand this and ensure that your board keeps proper records and follows proper processes and procedures.

Although in most cases it will be the company that takes – or does not take – actions that put it at risk, there are certain circumstances when that risk can pass to the directors. It is important that you take steps to ensure that you are aware of such risks and protect yourself by properly considering the implications of decisions and by keeping proper minuted records of both the board's considerations and their decisions.

If you disagree with a decision, even if you are outvoted, you can still be liable for the results. Make sure that your objection is recorded!

Your biggest risk is likely to be financial. The board must ensure that it can reasonably expect to be able to pay its creditors. The board must be constantly vigilant about wrongful trading, overtrading or trading fraudulently.

It is an offence for a company to continue to trade while insolvent. Further, it is also an offence to enter into an agreement where doing so would result in the company becoming insolvent; if it does, then the directors can become personally liable for those debts incurred after the date that it became insolvent.

Should a company get into financial difficulties the board is expected to minimise creditors' losses, and should take legal and/or financial advice on the best and most prudent courses of action.

As a director you should at all times be able to demonstrate that the board has been exercising reasonable care, skill and diligence and that the directors have had regard to the likely consequences of any decision in the long term.

Directors can also be liable if the company fails to implement proper processes covering:

- Health and safety
- Employment law
- Control and disposal of hazardous waste

In the UK a director may also be liable for failure by the company to make required filings at Companies House.

You can mitigate these risks by taking out professional indemnity insurance and learning to become a professional and effective director. Further, you should exercise your right to obtain professional advice, either from company officers or independent professionals.

You can take on the liabilities of a director unknowingly by becoming what is known as a 'shadow director' if the directors of a limited company are accustomed to acting in accordance with your directions or instructions. However, professional advisors giving advice in their professional capacity are specifically excluded from the definition of a shadow director in UK companies legislation. Make sure that you are clear about your status.

Why people do become directors

Appointment as a director can be a natural stage in your career development and an exceedingly rewarding activity.

Directors are involved in an organisation at a higher, more strategic level. They have greater leverage and can make a greater contribution.

It can also, of course, be financially rewarding; you should expect some compensation for your expertise, experience and the additional risk that you take on.

The Memorandum & Articles

The constitution of a company comprises two documents:

1. the Memorandum of Association
2. the Articles of Association

The memorandum of association is the document that sets up the company and the articles of association sets out how the company is run, governed and owned.

Memorandum of Association

Under the United Kingdom Companies Act 2006 the memorandum of association is a legal statement signed by all initial shareholders confirming they agree to form the company and take at least one share. The exact wording of the statement can't be changed later.

Historically, a company's memorandum of association contained an objects clause, which limited its capacity to act. When the first limited companies were incorporated, the objects clause had to be widely drafted so as not to restrict the board of directors in their day-to-day trading. In the Companies Act 1989 the term "General Commercial Company" was introduced which meant that companies could undertake "any lawful or legal trade or business", except that charitable companies must state the charitable objects that the company is restricted to and community interest companies must restrict the company to objects that benefit the community.

Articles of Association

The Articles of Association is now the single constitutional document for a UK company, and subsume the role previously filled by the separate memorandum of association.

The Articles of Association is a document that contains the purpose of the company as well as the duties and responsibilities of its members defined and recorded clearly. It is an important document that, in the UK, needs to be filed with the Registrar of Companies.

The Articles set out the rules for running the company. It is important, therefore, that directors should study the articles of their company. Typically the articles will contain regulations covering the following areas, together with many more minor matters:

- Company name
- Proposed location of the company's registered office

- Object of the company
- Statement regarding liability of its members
- Detail of the company's share capital
- Name of each individual shareholder
- Rules for the company's internal regulation and management
- Meeting procedures
- Powers of directors
- Members' rights
- Procedure for paying dividends

If the company is to be a non-profit making company, the Articles will contain a statement saying that the profits shall not be distributed to the members.

The Articles can be amended by a resolution formally approved by a meeting of the company's members.

Directors, shareholders and managers

Although any one individual might be both director, shareholder and manager, these are distinct, different roles representing different interests.

To be both effective and ethical, it is important to recognise 'which hat you are wearing' at any one time.

Many directors might also be shareholders, in some case significant or even majority shareholders. All directors are appointed by and represent the shareholders; loyalty is to the organisation and to the shareholders as a whole.

Executive directors by definition have an executive role within the organisation. Most probably they have a management role, but it might be as an internal advisor or specialist. All directors are expected to bring their knowledge and experience to the board executive directors must recognise their responsibility for the good of the organisation as a whole and not any individual department or personal self interest.

When acting in a board capacity, directors' responsibility is to the organisation and they must make sure they are able to separate themselves from any other interest or role. Where they cannot do this, they must 'declare an interest', which should be minuted, and probably withdraw from the discussions.

If directors are employees or represent suppliers or significant customers, then they are stakeholders as well. Companies are increasingly expected to take account of the needs of stakeholders, including the local community and the environment. It is the role of the board to balance various interests with the long term interest of the company.

Functions of a board

The board of directors has three primary functions:

- Stewardship of the company, its employees and its resources
- Fiduciary duty to its shareholders*
- Compliance with legislation and regulation

*Whereas the directors of a viable company have a duty to operate the company in the interests of the shareholders, this changes when doubts arise over the ability of the firm to continue as a going concern. Both executive and non-executive directors must then pay increasing regards to the interests of creditors.

Good boards are focused, results-oriented and disciplined. Agendas and committee structures focus on strategic primacy and value creation.

The main board is responsible for the success of the company within a framework of controls, which enables risk to be assessed and managed. It is responsible for setting strategy, maintaining the policy and decision making framework in which this strategy is implemented, ensuring that the necessary financial and human resources are in place to meet strategic aims, monitoring performance against key financial and non-financial indicators, overseeing the system of risk management and for setting values and standards in governance matters.

Directors are not appointed to micro-manage an organisation, but rather for oversight, insight and foresight. In terms of their oversight function, directors must ensure that appropriate processes and controls are in place to manage and monitor risks and to provide for smooth, effective and efficient functioning of the business.

With respect to insight, directors are there to add their experiences and wisdom, not to second-guess management but to supplement and enhance executive decision-making.

As for foresight, the directors are there to provide a perspective on the future that helps management identify those opportunities that are most worth pursuing.

Directors should be constructively involved in the development and approval of strategy; their involvement should be seen as cooperative rather than adversarial. At the core of constructive involvement is the role they perform through the questions they ask. By asking questions, directors determine both the degree to which the organisation is on a proper course and whether it is being properly managed.

Board composition

The minimum and maximum size of a board is usually determined by the company's articles, which may be changed by the members' meeting.

The size of a board will influence its style. Small boards tend to act cohesively: large boards may find sectional interests and cliques developing, and there may be a call for standing committees to handle matters of detail.

Company size by turnover	Average number of directors
Up to £50m	8
£50m - £100m	8
£100m - £500m	9
Over £500m	12

Typical board composition

But of more importance than the absolute size of the board is its structure – the balance between interests, experience and backgrounds represented.

The way the board is structured has implications for corporate governance and the work of the director. The key distinction is between executive directors, who are also managers, and non-executive or outside directors, who are not. Boards can vary considerably in the balance between the two.

Board structure

The all-executive board

At one extreme is the all-executive board. This form is quite common in wholly-owned subsidiaries and private companies and is not unknown in plcs. In effect the entire top management team, or part of it, forms the board.

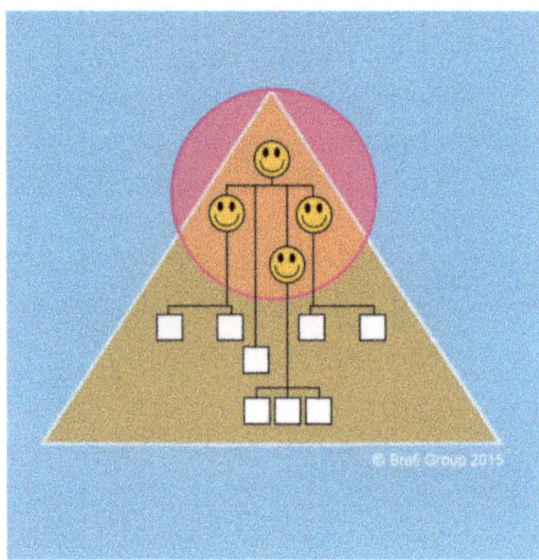

There are no outside directors.

Appointment of non-executive directors

As private companies grow they will recognise the benefit of inviting outsiders to become non-executive directors and contribute both an independent view and a combination of expertise, experience and contacts.

Sometimes in group companies non-executive directors are appointed to the boards of subsidiaries from elsewhere in the group. For example, the chair of the board may be a head office executive or a main board director.

Typical board structure in a British public company

In a typical British company you might find approximately half the directors, including the chairman, are non-executive.

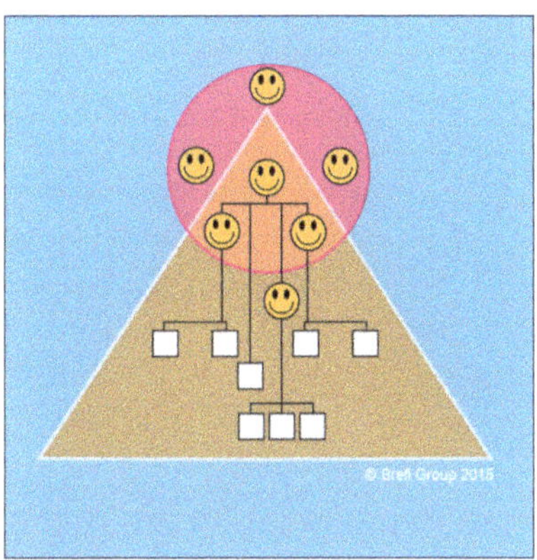

Typical US board structure

By contrast, the public company in the United States is heavily weighted in favour of the non-executive as a means of providing wise counsel to the chief executive, whose operating officers are kept quite separate. It is likely to have a majority of independent outside directors, with only the chief executive and finance director being executives.

Whereas in Britain more than 90% of FTSE 100 companies have long separated the roles of chairman and CEO, in America it has been traditional for the roles to be combined. However, the trend is toward separate roles and by 2011 a record 44% of S&P 500 companies and 62% of NASDAQ 100 companies had done so.

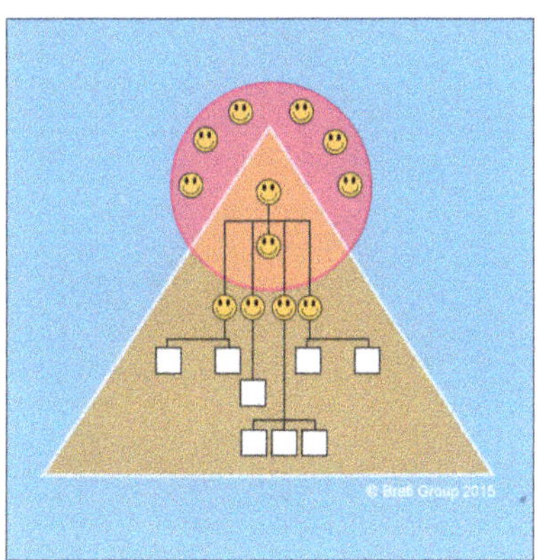

The theoretical purpose of the board is to hold the management accountable. However, Steve Jobs appointed directors to Apple's board as mentors who would support him and companies such as Facebook, Google and News Corp have shareholding structures that give the founders a controlling vote.

Board structure in a typical German company

The practice in some European companies, such as Germany, is a total separation between the executive board and the independent supervisory board. This is the two-tier board. The chief executive or general manager is not a member of the supervisory board but is available to attend its meetings if required.

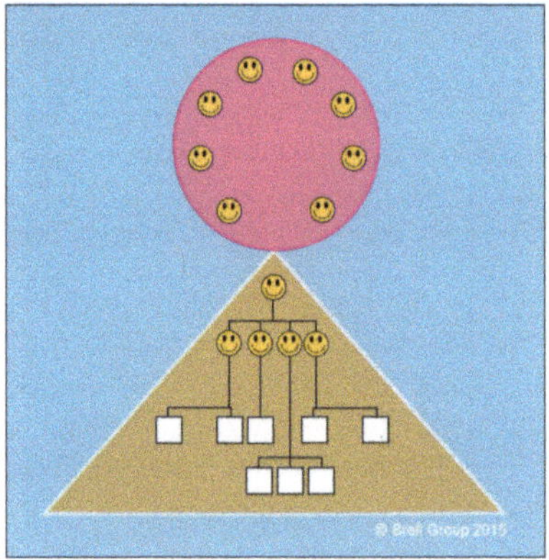

> The distinctive feature of these systems is that the shareholders have an opportunity to influence the composition of a body which has as its function the exercise of general and relatively continual control and supervision over the activities of those managing the company's affairs. The members of the supervisory body have the opportunity of scrutinising the management of the company on behalf of the shareholders in a way that the shareholders themselves, particularly small shareholders, usually cannot.
>
> European Commission *Fifth Directive* 1972

Groups of companies

Most major businesses these days operate as a group of companies.

There are important implications for directors of companies in a group as their boards are likely to include directors representing different interests.

A group of companies exists where one company owns a controlling interest in another; that is, it has sufficient shares to give it a voting majority and is able to determine the appointment of directors and effectively influence the policy and strategy.

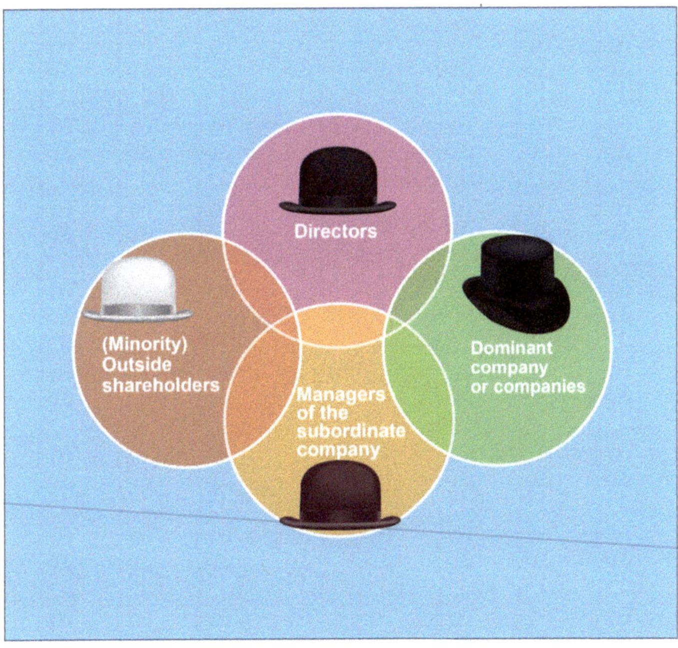

A subsidiary company is one in which all, or a majority, of the voting shares are held by another company. If the parent owns all the shares, the subsidiary is wholly-owned. If the parent holds less than 100% of the voting shares, there are minority shareholders whose rights have to be recognised and protected. This is a duty of the subsidiary company.

In an associate company another company holds a significant proportion of the shares, without holding a clear majority, but sufficient to exercise power over the board membership and corporate policy. Directors of an associate company need to be sensitive to the balance of power among the shareholders.

A holding company is one that is at the head of a group, its own shares being held by individuals or financial institutions, no single one of which exercises a dominant power. The board of the holding company determine the direction of the group for the benefit of the members, and are not themselves dependent on a company board at a higher level. The board of the holding company is responsible to the shareholders at the annual general meeting.

Implications for directors

In some cases the parent company may act as a remote, financial-oriented holding company, looking for dividends and capital growth as the periodic benefit from their group company – leaving the board of the subsidiary to run a relatively independent business. In other cases the corporate structure may be no more than a legal convenience. Management control will be exercised through the management organisation structure. Moreover, this management system may not even be congruent with the corporate legal structure. In such cases power lies with the management stream of head office executives, divisional and unit executives: little real power is held at the subsidiary board level.

Nevertheless, the legal responsibilities of the directors of these group companies must be fulfilled. This is particularly important when there are minority shareholders of the subsidiary. The boards of such companies must make sure that decisions are taken for the benefit of all the shareholders, including the minority; their rights must not be lost sight of in the group decision-making.

Types of director

Chairman

The chairman creates the conditions for overall board and individual director effectiveness. With the help of the executive directors and the company secretary, the chairman sets the agenda for the board's deliberations and ensures that strategy, performance, value creation and accountability, and issues relevant to these areas are reserved for board decision.

It is the responsibility of the chairman to:

- Create a climate in which thought and expression may flourish naturally
- Bring both individual and collective views together in a cohesive form
- Ensure awareness of what has been decided

The chairman also ensures effective communication with shareholders and other stakeholders and, in particular, that all directors are made aware of the views of those who provide the company's capital.

The chairman of each board committee fulfils an important leadership role similar to that of the chairman of the board, particularly in creating the conditions for overall committee and individual director effectiveness.

Senior Independent Director

The boards of publicly listed companies should appoint a senior independent director from among their independent non-executives. To qualify as "independent", non-executives need to have the necessary independence of character and judgement and also be free of any connections that may lead to a conflict of interest. This means not having any contractual or other relationship with the company or its directors apart from the current office of director and not being subject to any control or influence of a third party which could affect the exercise of independent judgement.

Senior independent directors serve as a sounding board for the chairman and act as an intermediary for the other directors. They are responsible for holding annual meetings with non-executives, without the chairman present, to appraise the chairman's performance. They would also be expected to meet with the non-executives on other such occasions when necessary.

When the board is undergoing a period of stress, the senior independent director's role becomes vitally important. He or she is expected to work with the chairman and the other directors, and/or shareholders, to resolve major issues. For example, they can act as an alternative point of contact for investors who may have made little headway in discussions with the chairman, chief executive or finance director – or who may have concerns about the performance of these individuals. Where the relationship between the chairman and chief executive is particularly close, and they do not communicate fully with shareholders, the senior independent director is able to step in and provide a link.

Where there is a disagreement or dispute between the chairman and the chief executive, the senior independent director can intervene, identify issues that have caused the rift and try to mediate and build a consensus.

Lead director

The lead-director role in America has grown out of amendments to the New York Stock Exchange listing requirements to require listed companies to have non-management directors meet at regularly scheduled executive sessions without management, overseen by a "presiding" director. This requirement combined with the increasing trend and pressure to increase board independence and separate the chairman and CEO roles led to the popularity of the independent lead-director role.

Many see it as an alternative to having a separate, independent chairman and accordingly attribute most of those responsibilities to the lead-director position. In its most basic form, the lead director is charged with leading the board's independent directors to engagement and consensus, ensuring that independent consensus is heard and implemented.

Executive director

Executive directors have the same duties as other members of the board. These duties extend to the whole of the business, and not just that part of it covered by their individual executive roles.

Most probably they have a management role, but it might be as an internal advisor or specialist.

Executive directors have the most intimate knowledge of the company and its capabilities when developing and presenting proposals, and when exercising judgements, particularly on matters of strategy. They should appreciate that constructive challenge from non-executive directors is an essential aspect of good governance, and should encourage their non-executive colleagues to test their proposal in the light of the non-executives' wider experience outside the company. The chairman and the CEO should ensure that this process is properly followed.

Chief Executive (CEO)

The chief executive is the most senior executive director on the board, with responsibility for proposing strategy to the board and for delivering the strategy as agreed. Their role is one of implementation; to implement board policy and report to the board on all aspects of that policy implementation.

They are accountable to the chairman and the board and is responsible for the management of the company within the guidelines laid down by the board, to which the CEO will also contribute.

The chief executive is responsible for devising the most appropriate management structure for the company and for recruiting, managing, motivating and retaining an effective management team, paying due regard to the needs of the future. It is up to them to communicate the company's values and behaviour right through the company.

They should ensure that the board is provided with the reports and information it needs, both to monitor company performance and to take those decisions that are its collective responsibility.

The CEO's relationship with the chairman is a key relationship that can help the board be more effective; the differing responsibilities of the chairman and CEO should be set out in writing and agreed by the board. The CEO is responsible for supporting the chairman to make certain that appropriate standards of governance permeate through all parts of the organisation.

Company Secretary

In the UK all public companies are obliged to have a company secretary; private companies are no longer required to do so, unless their articles of association explicitly require them to.

In a public company, the directors must make sure, as far as is reasonably possible, that the secretary has "the requisite knowledge and experience to discharge the functions of secretary of the company" and has the requisite qualifications, such as chartered accountant or chartered secretary.

They are responsible for maintaining the company's statutory registers and books, and filing annual returns. They arrange meetings of the company's directors and shareholders and ensure proper notices of meetings are issued; they prepare agendas, circulate relevant papers and take and produce minutes to record the business transacted at the meetings and the decisions taken.

The obligations and responsibilities of the company secretary necessitate them playing a leading role in the good governance of companies by supporting the chairman and helping the board and its committees to function efficiently.

The company secretary should report to the chairman on all board governance matters. This does not preclude them from also reporting to the CEO in relation to his or her other executive management responsibilities.

The appointment and removal of the company secretary should be a matter for the board as a whole, and the remuneration of the company secretary might be determined by the remuneration committee.

Chief Financial Officer (CFO)

The chief financial officer has a particular responsibility to deliver high quality information to the board on the financial position of the company.

Non-executive director

Non-executive directors bring experience and judgement to the deliberations of the board that the executive directors on their own would lack.

Non-executive directors should, on appointment, devote time to a comprehensive, formal and tailored induction, which should extend beyond the boardroom and include visiting and talking with senior and middle managers of the main business areas.

Non-executive directors should take into account the views of shareholders and other stakeholders, because these views may provide different perspectives on the company and its performance.

The New York Stock Exchange has recommended that a framework should be established to allow non-executive directors to meet at regularly scheduled executive sessions without management, as a means of promoting open discussion among themselves without any influence or pressure from executive directors.

The independent directors must designate, and publicly disclose the name of, the director who will preside at the executive sessions.

In contrast to executives, non-executive directors are normally remunerated on a fixed-fee basis. This is to ensure that non-executives retain an objective and independent perspective on the activities of the company. For this reason, share options would not normally form part of a non-executive's remuneration framework.

Nominee director

A nominee director is one who acts as a non-executive director on the board of a company on behalf of another person or firm such as a bank, investor, or lender.

Nominee directors carry the same responsibilities, and risks, as other directors.

Nominee directorships can sometimes be useful, for example in preparing "off-the-shelf" ready-made companies. But the nominee system can be used to disguise control and is open to abuse if the nominee secretly hands back all control to the real owner. In many such cases they are residents of tax havens acting on behalf of non-residents as a trustee on the board of an off-shore firm in that haven.

Shadow director

A shadow director is a person in accordance with whose directions or instructions the directors of a company are accustomed to act. Under this definition, it is possible that a director, or the whole board, of a holding company, and the holding company itself, could be treated as a shadow director of a subsidiary.

A founder or significant shareholder who wishes to escape the disclosure requirements of a directorship might still be counted as a 'shadow' director and held responsible for actions as if he or she were a formal director.

Professional advisors giving advice in their professional capacity are specifically excluded from the definition of a shadow director in UK companies legislation.

Tunjic Directorship Model

In this model Peter Tunjic differentiates between the roles of the board and of management, and between the board responsibilities for strategy and for compliance.

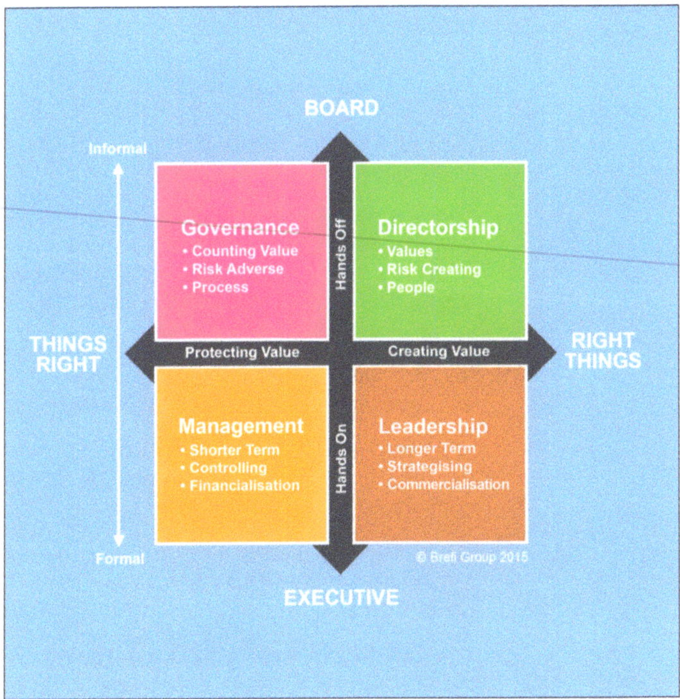

With the current focus on corporate governance there is a danger of organisations being over governed and under directed, with too much focus on ensuring the "correct" board structure, process and composition rather than imagination, creativity, or ethical behaviour.

To give them the best chance of success they need the right combination of leading, managing, governing and directing.

Directors and managers do different things. But when they 'govern' and 'manage' they approach those tasks with the same mindset of *doing things right*. Likewise, when directors direct their attitude should be that of a leader – *doing the right things*.

Governance and leadership are states of mind. Only managers manage and directors direct; but leadership and governance can be practised throughout the firm.

Delegation to management

You are a director. You might be a manager in the same organisation.

It is *really* important to recognise that these are different roles: you must act as two different people.

If you are a director and not a manager in the same organisation, then you have to understand the boundaries between the board and the management.

Directors direct – and managers manage!

Nonetheless, the board is responsible for the management's actions and performance.

The board remains responsible for overall governance. This includes ensuring senior management establish and maintain adequate systems of risk management and that the level of capital held is consistent with the risk profile of the organisation.

So, the board needs to have a clear strategy of what to delegate to management and how to monitor and evaluate the implementation of policies, strategies and business plans.

The responsibility to act and decide upon matters for action in between meetings of the board may be delegated to an executive committee.

In general the board will delegate the management of the organisation to the Chief Executive Officer (CEO) or Managing Director (MD).

The CEO/MD is responsible for delivering services according to the strategic plan, within the policies and budgets approved by the board. A team of managers oversees the day-to-day operations of the organisation under the general direction of the CEO/MD.

Delegation to committees

Boards have a limited amount of time for meetings, and so the Articles of Association normally permit the board to delegate its functions to committees of the board. There is normally no limitation on what the board can choose to delegate to committees.

Committees are often a means of utilising the expertise of non-executive directors and of involving them more in the organisation's affairs.

If you are invited to join a board you should enquire as to these extra responsibilities and potential calls on your time.

In the UK, the Cadbury and Hampel Committees recommended that boards should set up a number of key sub-committees with specific responsibilities, in particular, audit, remuneration and nomination committees. These committees are committees of the board; the board agrees their terms of reference and their membership; the board retains the responsibility for committee decisions and makes the final decision on all of these areas.

These committees are also required under London Stock Exchange listing rules.

Sufficient time should be allowed after committee meetings for them to report to the board on the nature and content of discussion, on recommendations, and on actions taken. The minutes of committee meetings should be circulated to all board members, unless it would be inappropriate to do so, and to the company secretary. The chairman of the board should ensure sufficient time is allowed at the board for discussion of these issue.

The remit of each committee, and the processes of interaction between committees and between each committee and the board, should be reviewed regularly.

Nomination Committee

The role of the nomination committee is to evaluate the balance of skills, knowledge and experience of the board, as well as amongst top management, to lead the process for board appointments and make recommendations to the board. In the light of this evaluation it will prepare a description of the role and capabilities required for a particular board appointment, and propose a management succession plan.

A majority of the members should be independent non-executive directors.

The chairman of the committee should be the chairman of the board or an independent non-executive director.

Audit Committee

The audit committee plays a particularly important role in the monitoring and oversight of larger companies. The main responsibilities of the audit committee include the following:

- To monitor the integrity of the financial statements of the company
- To review the company's internal controls and risk management systems
- To monitor and review the effectiveness of the company's internal audit function
- To make recommendations to the board in relation to the appointment or removal of the external auditor
- To approve the remuneration and terms of engagement of the external auditor
- To review and monitor the external auditor's independence and effectiveness
- To develop and implement policy on the engagement of the external auditor to supply non-audit services
- To review the risk situation, and to monitor risk-management processes.

Given the relatively technical nature of the audit committee's activities, the board should satisfy itself that at least one member of the audit committee has recent and relevant financial experience. In practice, this is likely to mean that this individual has an accountancy qualification, and has gained relevant financial experience while working as an auditor or financial manager.

All members should be independent non-executive directors. Large companies should have at least three members. Smaller companies should have at least two members.

In companies in the FTSE 350, the chairman of the board should not be a member of the audit committee. In companies outside the FTSE 350, the chairman of the board may be a member of the audit committee if he or she was considered independent when first appointed as chairman.

The audit committee should also review arrangements by which staff of the company may, in confidence, raise concerns about possible improprieties in matters of financial reporting or other matters.

Remuneration committee

In order to avoid conflicts of interest, executive directors should not be responsible for determining their own remuneration.

The UK Corporate Governance Code recommends that boards should establish a remuneration committee of at least three, or in the case of smaller companies two, independent non-executive directors. In addition the company chairman may also be a member of, but may not chair, the committee if he or she was considered independent on appointment as chairman.

The remuneration committee is delegated responsibility for proposing the remuneration of all executive directors, including pension rights and any compensation payments. The committee should also define and monitor the level and structure of remuneration for senior management.

The remuneration committee should make available its terms of reference, explaining its role and the authority delegated to it by the board. Where remuneration consultants are appointed, a statement should be made available of whether they have any other connection with the company.

In the case of companies listed on the London Stock Exchange, shareholders should be invited specifically to approve all new long-term incentive schemes and significant changes to existing schemes, save in the circumstances permitted by the Listing Rules.

The remuneration committee should carefully consider what compensation commitments (including pension contributions and all other elements) their directors' terms of appointment would entail in the event of early termination. The aim should be to avoid rewarding poor performance. They should take a robust line on reducing compensation to reflect departing directors' obligations to mitigate loss.

The annual report and accounts of a listed company should include a report to shareholders by the remuneration committee, containing various disclosures about directors' remunerations, a statement that full consideration has been given to best practice relating to remunerations policy and a statement of compliance with the best practice provisions of the Greenbury Report.

Other committees

Boards may establish an executive committee to manage its business between board meetings. If so, its powers and responsibilities should be clearly specified.

They may also establish other committees, but the value and benefits of establishing an elaborate committee structure need to be carefully considered.

Other committees might include, a finance committee, a planning committee, as well as human resources, donations, environmental compliance, health and safety, intellectual property. These will depend on such considerations as the character of the organisation, market conditions, regulations and the litigation environment.

Finance Committee

This committee is responsible for recommending financial policies, goals, and budgets that support the mission, values, and strategic goals of the organisation. The committee also reviews the organisation's financial performance against its goals and proposes major transactions and programmes to the board.

It is able to review and recommend capital expenditures and unbudgeted operating expenditures that exceed management's spending authority but are below the threshold required for board approval.

It might also recommend policies governing investments and pension plans and approve the selection of independent investment advisers and managers.

Check out your behaviour now

Check out your behaviour and what you have learned against the corporate governance checklists in Chapter 16.

Find out more about director development and corporate governance at: www.corporatedirector.co.uk

3. Before Accepting a Directorship

Do you really want to become a director?

Before you accept an invitation to join a board, you should consider whether you really wish to become a director.

Firstly, it is as well to be aware of any restrictions on you becoming a director:

- In the UK you must be over 16 years old
- You cannot also be the company's auditor
- You must not be an undischarged bankrupt
- You must not be disqualified from being a director by a court order

In addition, there might be relevant government regulations or restrictions in the company's Articles of Association that disqualify you from being a director of this particular company.

Next, you should seriously consider the time commitment. How often does the board meet? Would you be required, maybe later, to take on more responsibilities, such as joining a committee or working party?

As a guide, you should reckon on 3-5 hours for each meeting and then allow three times that time for preparation; for a director of a large company this could amount to 300 hours a year. For you to be effective, you must be prepared to study board papers and find linkages and inconsistencies. You might need to follow up and clarify some of the information, or do some external research as part of your preparation.

Check out the culture and relationships of this board

Creating business value is increasingly the job of a human social system – the board – in which no one holds individual formal power. That's very different from the hierarchy of corporate management and you should consider how you will prepare yourself for this.

Different boards will have different cultures – their unspoken norms of behaviour – that are critical to a company's success. Before deciding to join a particular board you should carry out your own exercise of due diligence.

Partly, this is about whether you will enjoy working on it. What are the other directors like? Do you share their values and aspirations for the company?

How do they operate as a board? Do they have good processes? Are discussions relevant, rigorous and penetrating? Do a few dominant directors commandeer the meeting? Are there factions? Does superficial knowledge go unchallenged? Is the chemistry collaborative? Is the board equipped to handle corporate life-threatening issues?

Do directors think, question and challenge, or are board meetings ritualistic, with tick box governance, inadequate understanding and a focus on short term and internal issues?

How do they deal with challenge, risk and conflict? Do they demonstrate curiosity to question and the courage to challenge? Are they alert to risks and the reality of what is happening around them; do they think for themselves?

Are they people of integrity, willing to ask difficult questions and are they there to make a contribution – or flatter their egos?

What is the relationship between the board and the management, between executive directors and non-executives?

You should certainly raise these sorts of questions with the chairman and meet as many of the current directors as possible.

You should ask for and read the last two years' worth of board minutes. These will give you an excellent insight into both the culture and the processes.

Remember, once appointed, you will be liable for the board's decisions from the day that you join – even if you miss a meeting.

Due diligence for directors

Before accepting a directorship you would be wise to carry out rigorous due diligence, just as you would before purchasing the company.

Prospective non-executive directors have a particular challenge as they are likely to have very limited previous knowledge about the company and its affairs. The UK's Institute of Chartered Secretaries and Administrators suggests a series of questions as the basis for personal analysis:

The business

- What is the company's current financial position and what has its financial track record been over the last three years?
- What are the exact nature and extent of the company's business activities?
- What is the company's competitive position and market share in its main business areas?
- What are the key dependencies (e.g. regulatory approvals, key licences)?

Governance and investor relations

- What record does the company have on corporate governance issues?
- Does the company have sound and effective systems of internal controls?
- Who are the current chief executive and non-executive directors, what is their background and record and how long have they served on the board?
- What is the size and structure of the board and board committees and what are the relationships between the chairman and the board, the chief executive and the management team?
- Who owns the company; who are the main shareholders and how has the profile changed over recent years?
- What is the company's attitude towards, and relationship with, its shareholders?

The role of the non-executive director

- Is the company clear and specific about the qualities, knowledge, skills and experience that it needs to complement the existing board?
- If the company is not performing particularly well is there potential to turn it round and do you have the time, desire and capability to make a positive impact?
- Are you satisfied that the size, structure and make-up of the board will enable you to make an effective contribution?
- Would accepting this non-executive directorship put you in a position of having a conflict of interest?

- Do you have the necessary knowledge, skills, experience and time to make a positive contribution to the board of this company?
- How closely do you match the job specification and how well will you fulfil the board's expectations?

Risk management

- Is there anything about the nature and extent of the company's business activities that would cause you concern in terms of risk and any personal ethical considerations?
- Is any material litigation presently being undertaken or threatened, either by the company or against it?
- Are you satisfied that the internal regulation of the company is sound and that you can operate within its stated corporate governance framework?
- What insurance cover is available to directors and what is the company's policy on indemnifying directors?

Sources of information

- Company report and accounts, and/or any listing prospectus, for the recent years
- Analysts' reports
- Press reports
- Company web site
- Any corporate social responsibility or environmental report issued by the company
- Rating agency reports
- Voting services reports

Exposure to risk

Companies have limited liability. This protects directors and shareholders, except when they hold partly paid shares; in which case they can be called upon to pay the outstanding sum. Loan capital is not protected and in smaller companies directors are sometimes asked to guarantee loans to the company, which puts them at risk if the loan conditions are not fulfilled.

If a company gets into financial difficulties, the board should seek professional advice immediately. If the company carries on trading to the detriment of its creditors – a practice known as wrongful trading – any director who should have concluded the "point of no return" had been reached, can be held personally liable for the debts if the company then goes into liquidation. Directors must therefore be aware of the company's financial status and ensure that someone competent monitors its solvency.

However, a director can be cleared of this liability if a court is satisfied that when the director realised that the company was not able to recover, he or she took reasonable steps to minimise potential losses to creditors.

Should doubts arise about the ability of the company to continue as a going concern, the directors must pay increasing regard to the interests of creditors. As well as seeking timely advice from specialist advisers, it is essential that directors in such circumstances raise concerns with the rest of the board and document their actions.

Factors that might help convince a court that directors acted properly include making sure that the financial situation and trading prospects were properly considered and:

- The board was properly constituted
- Board meetings took place with a detailed agenda of what was to be discussed
- Board meetings were properly minuted
- Proper information was provided and records kept

Similar risks apply for corporate manslaughter and, potentially, for environmental damage. The board must be able to demonstrate that it has implemented and monitored appropriate processes to protect employees, the public and the environment from harm. In many countries there is additional risk from accusations of bribery, either institutional or by a rogue employee.

If a director is successfully sued for damages, he or she may claim a contribution from anyone else who is also found to be responsible. However, a court can lift this liability wholly or partially if it is satisfied that the director acted honestly and reasonably and, on balance, ought fairly to be excused.

On becoming a director you should ensure that the company has obtained appropriate 'Director's Indemnity' insurance – or obtain your own. Directors should also have the right to professional advice from within the company or externally should they request it.

Should a director conclude that the company is behaving inappropriately, he or she might feel tempted to resign. However, this does not necessarily free them from their obligation and liabilities.

Directors must be seen to have taken positive steps to do everything they could to ensure that the magnitude of a company's problems – or their perception of them – is brought to the attention of the full board of directors.

Directors should also try to make sure that the company takes all the steps necessary, including seeking professional advice, to try to recover.

Check out your behaviour now

Check out your behaviour and what you have learned against the corporate governance checklists in Chapter 16.

Find out more about director development and corporate governance at: www.corporatedirector.co.uk

4. Corporate Governance and the Role of the Board

What is corporate governance?

According to the OECD:

> "Corporate governance is the system by which business corporations are directed and controlled. The corporate governance structure specifies the distribution of rights and responsibilities among different participants in the corporations such as the board, managers, shareholders and other stakeholders, and spells out the rules and procedures for making decisions on corporate affairs."

The UK Corporate Governance Code defines it as follows:

> "Corporate Governance is the system by which companies are directed and controlled. The boards of directors are responsible for the governance of their companies. The shareholders' role in governance is to appoint the directors and auditors and to satisfy themselves that an appropriate governance structure is in place. The responsibilities of the board include setting the company's strategic aims, providing the leadership to put them into effect, supervising the management of the business and reporting to shareholders on their stewardship. The board's actions are subject to laws, regulations and the shareholders in general meeting."

The King III report in South Africa explains good governance as:

> "Good governance is essentially about effective leadership. Leaders should rise to the challenges of modern governance. Such leadership is characterised by the ethical values of responsibility, accountability, fairness and transparency and based on moral duties that find expression in the concept of Ubuntu*. Responsible leaders direct company strategies and operations with a view to achieving sustainable economic, social and environmental performance."

*Ubuntu is a Nguni Bantu term roughly translating as "human kindness".

Corporate governance is about what the board of a company does and how it sets the values of the company. It is to be distinguished from the day to day operational management of the company by full-time executives.

Good governance is not just about compliance with formal rules and regulations. It is about establishing internal processes and attitudes that add value, enhance the reputation of a business, make it more attractive to external investors and lenders and ensure its long term success.

It is about the way in which boards oversee the running of a company by its managers, and how board members are in turn accountable to shareholders and the company. This has implications for company behaviour towards employees, shareholders, customers and banks. Good corporate governance plays a vital role in underpinning the integrity and efficiency of financial markets. Poor corporate governance weakens a company's potential and at worst can pave the way for financial difficulties and even fraud.

The purpose of corporate governance is to facilitate effective, entrepreneurial and prudent management that can deliver the long-term success of an organisation.

Corporate governance can be considered from two viewpoints: -

- Determining the organisation's vision, mission and values; developing and implementing strategy; and then reviewing performance in the context of the organisation's vision, mission and values, or;
- Adopting best practice as defined by respected external parties.

The responsibility to actively participate in the development and approval of the overall strategy, to monitor the strategy's progress, and to oversee and guide the organisation represents some of the quintessential activities of corporate governance. That responsibility resides principally with the board.

In its preface to the 2014 Corporate Governance Code, the UK Financial Reporting Council states that one of the key roles for the board includes establishing the culture, values and ethics of the company. It is important that the board sets the correct 'tone from the top'. The directors should lead by example and ensure that good standards of behaviour permeate throughout all levels of the organisation. This will help prevent misconduct, unethical practices and support the delivery of long term success.

According to the OECD, a corporate governance framework should consist of three main elements:

- A set of relationships between a company's management, its board, its shareholders and other stakeholders
- A structure through which the objectives of the company are set and the means of attaining those objectives and monitoring performance are determined
- Proper incentives for the board and management to pursue objectives that are in the interests of the company and its shareholders.

Comply or explain

The 'comply or explain' approach is the trademark of corporate governance in the UK. It has been in operation since the Cadbury Report in 1992. It is strongly supported by both companies and shareholders and has been widely admired and imitated internationally.

The purpose of 'comply or explain' is to let the market decide whether a set of standards is appropriate for individual companies. Since a company may deviate from the standard, this approach rejects the view that one size fits all, but because of the requirement of disclosure of explanations to market investors, anticipates that if investors do not accept a company's explanations, then investors will sell their shares, hence creating a 'market sanction', rather than a legal one.

In the Netherlands and South Africa they decided that the proper approach was to 'apply' instead of 'comply'.

Like the Dutch, the South Africans believe in giving entities the freedom to choose principles and practices that are applicable to their processes, as long as they can justify their decisions. The 'apply or explain' approach regime shows an appreciation for the fact that it is often not a case of whether to comply or not, but rather to consider how the principles and recommendations can be applied.

Although in the United States Sarbanes-Oxley regulations use the "comply or explain" method in some instances, in most instances US regulation tends to rely on the legislation and fines and imprisonment penalties for violating the requirements of SOX. This approach to corporate governance is known as 'comply or else'. All entities are expected to comply, no exceptions.

The King III Report pointed out that the Sarbanes-Oxley Act, with its inflexibility, had not prevented the collapse of many of the leading companies in the US banking and finance sector and had cost the USA US$264 billion since 2002.

Reasons why corporate governance matters

Good governance can be seen in the quality of decisions; effective decision making is based on hard information from robust systems and processes that are used effectively by leaders in a culture that supports challenge and scrutiny. Good governance helps mitigate or reduce risk and avoid scandals, fraud, and criminal liability of the company.

If companies are well governed, they will usually outperform other companies and will be able to attract investors whose support can help to finance further growth. Effective corporate governance attracts higher levels of investment. A survey by the International Finance Corporation, part of the World Bank, found that governance is an important factor in making investment decisions in emerging markets. In fact, investors will pay a premium for firms in emerging markets that can demonstrate better governance.

It is now accepted that sound governance results in better performing companies that deliver total economic value within its broader meaning and corporate governance is now established in many countries across the world.

A history of corporate governance

Corporate governance and compliance practices have undergone enormous change in a relatively short time and best practices are continually developing. The level of scrutiny of a board's monitoring – or failure to monitor – a corporation's ethics and compliance activities has increased dramatically. The challenge for boards, executive officers, and ethics and compliance officers is to view the increased scrutiny and enhanced standards not merely as a host of new legal requirements but as an opportunity to review and enhance their corporate governance and ethics and compliance practices and set a true tone from the top.

Development of corporate governance in the UK

The concept of formalised best practice in corporate governance was originally developed in the United Kingdom, starting with the Cadbury Report, published in 1992, and is now integrated into the UK Corporate Governance Code.

The Code applies to all companies with a premium listing on the London Stock Exchange and the latest version is effective for financial years beginning on or after 1 October 2014.

The Code encourages smaller companies to adopt the approach set out in the Code.

The Cadbury Report (1992) looked into the performance and reward of boards and resulted in greater transparency and accountability in boardroom proceedings. It included a code of best practice with guidelines for behaviour and disclosure and also recommended that the board should have three non-executive directors and an audit committee to oversee greater control of financial reporting and that the role of chairman and chief executive should be held by different people.

The Greenbury Report (1995) recommended appointment of a remuneration committee to determine directors' remuneration and a nominations committee to oversee new appointments to the board.

In 1998 the Hampel Committee reviewed the success of the Cadbury and Greenbury reports. Its report consolidated the recommendations of the two previous reports and recommended the creation of a 'Combined Code', which was annexed to the UK Stock Market's Listing Rules. It also made recommendations on improving communication with shareholders and redressing the balance between implementing controls and allowing companies to find their own ways of applying corporate governance principles.

The Turnbull report (1999) covered operational and financial controls based on high-level principles of good governance rather than rules or detailed checklists.

The main recommendations were that:

- boards should be required to make an annual statement on the effectiveness of internal controls
- boards, not operational managers, were responsible for risk management and internal control
- the guidance covered all internal controls, not just financial reporting, and takes a 'risk-based' approach
- the guidance was to assist, not restrict, how a company operates
- boards should continue to review application of the guidance, to embed the controls in how a company operates, with procedures to identify and report weaknesses
- companies should not need to develop new processes
- external auditors' responsibility over internal controls should not increase.

The Higgs Report (2003) reviewed the role and effectiveness of non-executive directors, including improved recruitment, appointment, induction and development, and formal terms of engagement.

It recommended that they should take on a more demanding and important role on company boards, comprise half the board, be drawn from a wider pool of candidates, be assessed annually, not serve more than two three-year terms on the board and meet as a group at least once a year without the chairman and the executive directors.

Before appointment, non-executive directors should conduct a due diligence exercise to satisfy themselves that they can make a positive contribution.

The Combined Code on Corporate Governance (2003) aimed to achieve more open and rigorous procedures for the appointment of directors and improved induction and development of non-executive directors. It recommended that half of the board members of FTSE 350 companies should be independent NEDs, that only NEDs should sit on the audit and remuneration committees and that if NEDs served more than nine years they were no longer considered to be independent (unlisted companies should have two NEDs on the board). The Code also called for formal evaluation – of boards, committees and individual directors.

The Code took a 'comply or explain' approach to encourage best practice in corporate governance. Listed companies were to report on how they had applied the principles in the Code, confirm that they complied with the Code's provisions or provide an explanation of any departures.

In July 2005 the Financial Reporting Council announced a review of the implementation of the Code which was published in January 2006 and an updated Code superseding and replacing the 2003 Code was published in July 2006.

The Tyson Report (2003) suggested that many UK companies would better represent and understand their customers, be better able to identify new markets and so become more competitive and productive if they widened their search for non-executive director talent and adopted rigorous and transparent recruitment procedures to include people with different backgrounds, including not-for-profit and non-commercial sectors, unlisted companies and private equity firms, business services and consultancies.

The UK Corporate Governance Code replaced the Combined Code in 2010 and introduced four new main principles:

- chairman's responsibility for leading the board
- need for directors to devote sufficient time
- requirement for NEDs to challenge constructively
- need for the board to have a balance of skills and experience.

One central change was the recommendation for the annual re-election of directors. Measures also included the promotion of balance and diversity in the composition of the board, in particular in relation to gender. It also addressed remuneration and how performance related pay for executive directors must have criteria to meet other than purely financial ones and must relate to the company's long term interests, risks and systems.

In 2010 the Institute of Directors and the European Confederation of Directors Associations published the Corporate Governance Guidance and Principles for Unlisted Companies in the UK. It recommended fourteen principles of good governance applicable on a voluntary basis. Nine of the principles apply to all unlisted companies and five are for large and/or complex unlisted companies. The focus is on establishing processes and adding value for long term success as shareholders of unlisted companies normally invest for the medium to long term and therefore transparency and accountability are vital. It can be seen as a governance roadmap for family run companies or entrepreneurs.

South Africa and the King reports

South Africa has emerged as a leader in the development of corporate governance with the work of Professor Mervyn King and his committees between 1994 and 2009. The latest version, known as King III, is the Code of and Report on Governance Principles for South Africa. The Institute of Directors in Southern Africa also sponsored the Code for Responsible Investing in South Africa 2011 (CRISA).

Whereas the King Code was written from the perspective of the board of the company, CRISA is intended to give guidance on how institutional investors should take account of sound corporate governance in their investment activities.

Read together, the King Code and CRISA provide a framework against which boards should benchmark their structure, processes and activities.

Unlike corporate governance codes such as Sarbanes-Oxley, the code is non-legislative, and is based on principles and practices. It also espouses an 'apply or explain' approach, unique to the Netherlands until recommended by the King Committee and now also found in the United Kingdom's Corporate Governance Code as 'comply or explain'.

The philosophy of the code consists of the three key elements of leadership, sustainability and good corporate citizenship. It views good governance as essentially being effective, ethical leadership. King believes that leaders should direct the company to achieve sustainable economic, social and environmental performance. It views sustainability as the primary moral and economic imperative of this century; the code's view on corporate citizenship flows from a company's standing as a juristic person under the South African constitution and should operate in a sustainable manner.

In the 2009 King III report, governance, strategy and sustainability were integrated. The report requires entities to submit an integrated report that reflects economic impact and achievements in sustainability. The Committee believes that financial reports don't offer the complete picture of what entities do. For example, it's not enough for companies to look out for their shareholders' best interests. They should also be able to report on and prove the positive impact they leave on the communities within which they operate.

In contrast to the earlier versions, King III is applicable to all entities, public, private and non-profit. King encourages all entities to adopt the King III principles and explain how these have been applied or are not applicable. The code of governance was applicable from March 2010.

Although the code of corporate governance is not enforced through legislation, due to evolutions in South African law, many of the principles put forward in King II are now embodied as law in the Companies Act of South Africa of 2008. In addition to the Companies Act, there are additional applicable statutes that encapsulate some of the principles of King III such as the Public Finance Management Act and the Promotion of Access to Information Act.

Corporate governance in the USA – Sarbanes-Oxley Act

In the United Sates, corporate governance is determined predominantly by legislation in the form of the Sarbanes-Oxley Act of 2002 ("SOX") and detailed regulations which SOX required the Securities and Exchange Commission, New York Stock Exchange and NASDAQ to draw up. It established a series of requirements that affect corporate governance in the USA and influenced similar laws in many other countries.

Sarbanes-Oxley was enacted to restore confidence in the markets after the collapse of the dot.com stock market boom and corporate governance scandals.

The Act requires CEOs and CFOs to confirm that the financial statements fairly represent financial decisions. They are also required to test and document the effectiveness of controls against financial reporting fraud and to make a public statement on the effectiveness of internal controls.

Board audit committees must have members that are independent and disclose whether or not at least one is a financial expert, or reasons why no such expert is on the audit committee.

External audit firms cannot provide certain types of consulting services and must rotate their lead partner every five years. Further, an audit firm cannot audit a company if those in specified senior management roles worked for the auditor in the past year.

SOX prohibited corporate loans to executives, required CEO certification of financial statements and bolstered regulation of audits and audit committees. The Dodd-Frank Act (2010) made it easier for dissident shareholders to nominate directors.

Small and medium-sized firms have no exemptions from the law and foreign companies listed in the United States also need to comply.

Corporate governance for unlisted companies

The duty to be accountable is particularly important in private and unlisted companies, especially if there are shareholders not involved in management whose interests need to be protected. In small companies owner-directors can often exercise considerable power and the board structure and the actions of the directors must recognise this.

Unlisted companies include start-ups, single owner-managed companies, family businesses, private equity-owned companies, joint ventures, subsidiary companies and many state-owned enterprises.

Unlisted companies are of particular importance in countries with less developed capital markets, where the vast majority of companies are not listed on a stock exchange or regulated market. Some family business owners may believe that attention to corporate governance is unnecessary because there is general agreement on the operation of the business and no one is looking over the shoulders of management to evaluate how things are done.

However, according to the OECD, improved corporate governance amongst unlisted companies has the potential to significantly boost productivity growth and job creation.

In recent years many countries have adopted corporate governance codes, most of which relate to listed companies. Copying the widely-recognised principles of best practice to listed companies is not necessarily a viable solution as the corporate governance challenges of listed companies are distinct from those of unlisted companies.

Listed companies often have large numbers of external minority shareholders and may be run by professional managers without significant ownership stakes. Unlisted companies are more likely to be owned and controlled by single individuals or coalitions of company insiders, with the owners continuing to play a significant role in management.

Good governance in this context is not a question of protecting the interests of absentee shareholders. Rather, it is concerned with establishing a framework of company processes and attitudes that add value to the business and help ensure its long-term continuity and success. Whereas much of the governance framework of listed companies may be externally imposed by various types of regulation and formal listing requirements, unlisted companies have greater scope to define – or not define – their own governance strategy.

Furthermore, they may not have access to in-house support to assist them in making important decisions about governance.

Corporate governance provides the framework within which decisions are made. Consequently, as a company seeks to improve the professionalism and sustainability of its activities, it needs to give greater thought to issues of governance. This is particularly relevant if it wants to move away from dependence on the unique contribution of the founding entrepreneur.

The development of effective governance processes may lift a significant burden from the founder, facilitate a swift succession and allow access to a wider pool of expertise and know-how, leading to improved leadership, decision-making and strategic vision.

Governance will also become an increasing issue for unlisted companies as they develop new sources of finance. A greater reliance on external funding from banks, venture capitalists and private equity investors will necessitate the implementation of a more explicit governance framework. The reward will be more stable financing at lower cost.

Investors in unlisted companies are likely to have to commit themselves to the company for the medium to longer term. An effective corporate governance framework provides shareholders with some reassurance that their interests will continue to be respected and safeguarded. As a result, they are more likely to invest in the first place and be a source of support for the company over the longer term.

Corporate governance for state owned enterprises

In spite of the recent trend to privatisation of nationalised industries, state-owned enterprises continue to play an important role in many countries. They are likely to be active in key sectors such as public utilities, infrastructure or energy and are major providers of employment, goods and services, ranging from the basic foodstuffs to military equipment.

Public ownership gives complete freedom in the choice of objectives and can therefore be used for any purpose that may be chosen. Whereas private ownership largely determines the ends for which it can be employed, the objectives under public ownership are undetermined and need to be consciously chosen.

It can be argued that state-owned enterprises should not be expected simply to outperform shareholder-owned enterprises but to evolve a more democratic and dignified system of industrial administration, a more humane employment of machinery, and a more intelligent utilisation of the fruits of human integrity and effort. Without the need for quarterly reports to shareholders they have a greater opportunity to incorporate long term and sustainable planning over short term gains.

It is important, therefore, that the pubic interest should be clearly defined, including the interests of the employees, the local and national community, the consumers, the suppliers and other state-owned enterprises.

Mixing business with politics risks producing inefficient business and corrupt politics. Directors should expect the organisation's charter to enumerate and define the rights, if any, which the minister or any other organs of government or parliament can exercise over the business side, and the rights and responsibilities of the board of directors. For example, the board might have to submit its business and financial plan to the relevant minister or government department and obtain approval for its budget.

Appointments to the board are less likely to be justified by commercial or technical experience than in the case of shareholder-owned companies. Although ministries should ensure they incorporate a range of field, professional and industry expertise at the board table, this is often lacking and directors who are under qualified and lack the necessary experience to evaluate, drive and enforce strategic direction are often appointed.

Directors appointed to state-owned enterprises should ensure that they understand what is expected of them, and are fully appraised of the legal basis for their role and any specific reporting requirements defined in legislation or government edict.

Here is an example of the challenge for directors in Russia

> *"In Russia, directors who are elected to the boards of state-owned companies are divided into two groups – independent directors and "professional attorney directors".*
>
> *The latter have to vote on a number of issues of board meetings agendas in accordance with instructions that are issued by the Federal State Property Management Agency. So, a professional attorney director has to vote on these issues even if personally he/she has a different opinion. They may outline their personal opinion in a special letter to be attached to the meeting minutes but the vote must be cast in accordance with the instruction.*
>
> *The other problem is that the state financial inspection bodies tend to accuse management and boards of state-owned enterprises of "inefficient decisions" and to launch legal prosecutions. So, when major transactions are discussed (sale or purchase of big assets, etc.) even independent directors elected by the shares owned by the state may prefer to ask for a vote instruction from the ministry that supervises this enterprises and this makes the decision-process much more bureaucratic."*
>
> Igor Belikov Director (CEO) at Russian Institute of Directors

The UK Corporate Governance Code

The UK Corporate Governance Code is the model that has been adopted or adapted in many countries.

It is not a rigid set of rules but consists of principles and provisions. The principles are the core of the Code and the way in which they are applied should be the central question for a board as it determines how it is to operate according to the Code.

The 'comply or explain' approach is the foundation of its flexibility and is strongly supported by both companies and shareholders, and has been widely admired and imitated internationally.

The main principles of the Code

Leadership

Every company should be headed by an effective board which is collectively responsible for the long-term success of the company.

There should be a clear division of responsibilities at the head of the company between the running of the board and the executive responsibility for the running of the company's business. No one individual should have unfettered powers of decision.

The chairman is responsible for leadership of the board and ensuring its effectiveness on all aspects of its role.

As part of their role as members of a unitary board, non-executive directors should constructively challenge and help develop proposals on strategy.

Effectiveness

The board and its committee should have the appropriate balance of skills, experience, independence and knowledge of the company to enable them to discharge their respective duties and responsibilities effectively.

There should be a formal and rigorous procedure for the appointment of new directors to the board.

All directors should be able to allocate sufficient time to the company to discharge their responsibilities effectively.

All directors should receive induction on joining the board and should regularly update and refresh their skills and knowledge.

The board should be supplied in a timely manner with information in a form and of a quality appropriate to enable it to discharge its duties.

The board should undertake a formal and rigorous annual evaluation of its own performance and that of its committees and individual directors.

All directors should be submitted for re-election at regular intervals, subject to continued satisfactory performance.

Accountability

The board should present a fair, balanced and understandable assessment of the company's position and prospects.

The board is responsible for determining the nature and extent of the principal risks it is willing to take in achieving its strategic objectives. The board should maintain sound risk management and internal control systems.

The board should establish formal and transparent arrangements for considering how they should apply the corporate reporting, risk management and internal control principles and for maintaining an appropriate relationship with the company's auditors.

Remuneration

Executive directors' remuneration should be designed to promote the long-term success of the company. Performance-related elements should be transparent, stretching and rigorously applied.

There should be a formal and transparent procedure for developing policy on executive remuneration and for fixing the remuneration packages of individual directors. No director should be involved in deciding his or her own remuneration.

Relations with shareholders

There should be a dialogue with shareholders based on the mutual understanding of objectives. The board as a whole has responsibility for ensuring that a satisfactory dialogue with shareholders takes place.

The board should use general meetings to communicate with investors and to encourage their participation.

Stakeholder engagement

In addition to financial success, companies are increasingly expected to address some of society's problems, including economic development, the environment and sustainability. As a result, companies are increasingly working with stakeholders to understand their views and concerns on various environmental, social, corporate governance and economic issues and to incorporate and address those views and concerns in the company's strategic decision-making processes.

Stakeholder engagement includes the formal and informal ways a company stays connected to its stakeholders. A primary objective of corporate stakeholder engagement is to build relationships with stakeholders to better understand their perspectives and concerns on key issues and to integrate those perspectives and concerns into the company's corporate strategy.

Boards should identify important stakeholder groups and ensure that management engages with them to ascertain legitimate expectations.

Companies tend to recognise value associated with stakeholder engagement, including:

- enabling informed board and management decision making;
- avoiding or reducing business risks due to better business intelligence;

- developing and expanding business opportunities, brand value and reputation; and
- bringing diverse perspectives together to facilitate innovation; all of which help drive long-term sustainability and shareholder value.

Corporate Social Responsibility

Increasingly, corporate social responsibility is seen as part of best practice by both investors and government. Most companies are keen to talk about social and environmental issues in their annual reports, and many argue that complying with CSR guidelines has become a commercial necessity: CSR builds trust, trust builds reputation, and reputation drives value.

Corporate social responsibility is defined by the European Commission as "the responsibility of enterprises for their impacts on society". The Commission encourages enterprises to "have in place a process to integrate social, environmental, ethical human rights and consumer concerns into their business operations and core strategy in close collaboration with their stakeholders".

The Association of British Insurers, whose members own more than 20 per cent of the companies on the London Stock Exchange, publishes guidance on CSR-related issues for both companies and investors. Its 2007 "Socially Responsible Investment Guidelines" asked that annual reports highlight company's environmental, social and governance (ESG) risks. A remuneration committee should also disclose whether it considers corporate performance on ESG issues when setting remuneration for senior executives, and whether an incentive structure may inadvertently encourage "irresponsible" ESG behaviour.

The UK Corporate Governance Code requires boards to set the company's values and standards and ensure that its obligations to its shareholders and others are understood and met, and the Turnbull Report makes clear that risk assessment should cover not only narrow financial risks but also those related to health, safety and environmental, reputation, and business probity issues.

The UK Companies Act 2006 requires directors to have regard to community and environmental issues when considering their duty to promote the success of their company.

The CSR report

The corporate social responsibility report (also commonly known as a corporate citizenship, sustainability or social performance report), due to the typical breadth of information most relevant to stakeholders' interests, can be a key component of a company's stakeholder engagement strategy.

As companies acknowledge the importance of stakeholder engagement, the use of corporate social responsibility reports has rapidly increased. A 2012 survey revealed that 53% of S&P 500 companies were reporting and disclosing CSR information, compared to approximately 20% of such companies in 2010.

Corporate CSR reports vary greatly in format, length and detail. There are, however, certain elements and disclosures that consistently appear in such reports. Those elements and disclosures include an opening letter from the company's chief executive officer and/or chief CSR executive, the company's CSR policy or mission statement, a 'forward-looking statements' disclaimer and disclosures addressing issues most important to each of the company's key stakeholders.

In a paper to the Harvard Law School Forum on Corporate Governance and Financial Regulation, Bill Libit, partner at Chapman and Cutler LLP, describes issues that could be included in a CSR report:

- **Shareholders** – addressing the company's business model and corporate governance, including disclosing the role of the board in risk management, in sustainability reporting and in evaluating CSR performance.
- **Employees** – addressing diversity, health and safety, training and mentoring, employee relations, and wages and benefits.
- **Customers** – addressing customer service and privacy.
- **Suppliers** – addressing labour standards and whether suppliers are required to implement their own CSR programmes.
- **Communities** – addressing corporate philanthropy and charitable contributions, community investment and partnerships, volunteerism and the environmental impact of operations.
- **Governments and regulators** – addressing lobbying, public policy and the effects of and compliance with environmental regulations.
- **Economic considerations** – disclosing the company's impacts on the economic conditions of its stakeholders and on economic systems at local, national and global levels.
- **Environmental issues** – disclosing the company's impacts on living and non-living natural systems (land, air, water and ecosystems), including impacts related to inputs

(such as energy and water), outputs (such as emissions, effluents and waste) as well as environmental compliance and expenditures.

- **Ethics and integrity** – disclosing the company's values, principles and standards, and its internal and external mechanisms for seeking advice on ethical and lawful behaviour and reporting concerns about unethical or unlawful behaviour and matters of integrity.
- **Social impact** – disclosing the company's impacts on the social systems within which it operates, including those relating to human rights, society and product responsibility.
- **Stakeholder engagement** – disclosing the company's stakeholder engagement during the reporting period and not limiting it solely to engagement conducted for purposes of preparing the CSR report.

Corruption

Companies are facing greater exposure to growth opportunities in emerging markets with a history of corruption. At the same time, there is a rising backlash against corporate wrongdoing by both protestors and governments in many developed and developing markets. Countries such as the United States, Germany, and the United Kingdom are strengthening and enforcing their own anticorruption and anti-bribery laws more vigorously, notably the US Foreign Corrupt Practices Act (FCPA) and the UK Bribery Act.

These efforts make companies increasingly liable not just for the conduct of their employees but also for the actions of their intermediaries, such as consultants, agents, and joint-venture partners.

Ravi Venkatesan, former chairman of Microsoft India and Cummins India and chairman of Social Venture Partners suggests that the hardest issues for ethical multinationals, regardless of their country of origin, are rarely the big-ticket scandals and scams that make headlines. Rather, it's the subtler but more pervasive forms of fraud and corruption, such as pressures for payments on routine transactions, that often pose the biggest challenge.

In an article for McKinsey & Company (2015) he identified four broad categories of corruption and fraud that executives are likely to come across – bribes, speed money, extortion, and employee fraud – and argued that companies should protect themselves against the risks by going beyond policies and controls and building a culture of ethics and compliance.

Too few foreign companies pay adequate attention to compliance, mainly because businesses usually allocate budgets for audits and compliance reviews in proportion to revenues rather than overall compliance risk.

The finance and administration unit is usually the primary contact with bureaucracy, and it's critical to have a strong team, with managers who understand local laws and regulations, possess the skills to work with government officials, and can get things done without paying bribes.

According to an Ernst & Young fraud survey, only 35 percent of companies had taken action against employees, and one-fifth of respondents stated that their companies did not have policies in place or they were unaware of an existing one.[2] In another survey, conducted by Kroll, less than one-third of respondents said their foreign employees, vendors, and managers were trained to be both familiar and compliant with the UK Bribery Act and the US FCPA.

Companies should institute a formal code of conduct that every employee has to recertify annually, with mandatory training on compliance and appropriate rules and regulations for customer-facing employees. Leaders should demonstrate their seriousness by paying attention to the small things with zero tolerance, swift investigation and punishment that is decisive and fair.

> *"It is not just a question of compliance. In my own experience, a strong adherence to corporate governance can be a potent competitive advantage when expanding abroad. At Gulftainer, a subsidiary of Crescent Enterprises, I have seen first-hand how an unwavering and zero-tolerance approach to corruption has helped the company in its drive to expand into new markets, including ones which to date score very badly on Transparency International's Corruption Perceptions Index."*
>
> Badr Jafar, Chief Executive, Crescent Enterprises, UAE

In hierarchical cultures, bribery and corruption depend largely on the tone from the top. Global companies should therefore hold their country CEOs accountable for compliance with their policies and codes of conduct, as well as with the laws of their host country.

Success is perfectly possible in emerging markets, claims Venkatesan, without making compromises, but there are real consequences and real costs for those who uphold ethical behaviour, especially in the short term; for example, some business may be lost, budgets may be missed, approvals may take more time, and officials may respond angrily. CEOs must ensure that every employee in every part of the world is utterly clear about what conduct is acceptable and what is not, and be prepared to explicitly acknowledge any loss of business that results from adherence to ethical principles.

> *"We ask our people to persist and prevail, not to take shortcuts. The message is simple: we will work alongside you. We will not hold it against you if a project gets delayed or we lose money; we will do what is right, not what is convenient. Over time, people will know what is acceptable here and what's not. Social memory is many times more effective than a bunch of policies."*
>
> Subroto Bagchi, Chairman of Mindtree Ltd, India

To combat the threat to their reputation – and ultimately to their bottom line – CEOs must make dealing with corruption a core employee and organisational competence. This requires a relentless focus on compliance, a commitment from senior leaders to ethical behaviour, and a determination to tough it out when these high standards appear to carry a short-term cost.

The OECD Anti-Bribery Convention 1997

The OECD Anti-Bribery Convention established legally binding standards to criminalise bribery of foreign public officials in international business transactions and provided for a host of related measures that make this effective. It was the first and only international anti-corruption instrument focused on the 'supply side' of the bribery transaction. The 34 OECD member countries and seven non-member countries – Argentina, Brazil, Bulgaria, Colombia, Latvia, Russia, and South Africa – have adopted the Convention.

The Convention deals with what, in the law of some countries, is called "active corruption" or "active bribery", meaning the offence committed by the person who promises or gives the bribe, as contrasted with "passive bribery", the offence committed by the official who receives the bribe.

The UK Bribery Act 2010

The Bribery Act 2010 was introduced in order to address the requirements of the 1997 OECD Anti-Bribery Convention and to update and enhance UK law on bribery, including foreign bribery. It presents heightened liability risks for companies, directors and individuals and reinforces the need for adequate systems and controls.

The Bribery Act introduces a new strict liability offence for companies and partnerships of failing to prevent bribery which, unlike previous legislation, places strict liability upon companies for failure to prevent bribes being given (active bribery); the only defence is that the company had in place adequate procedures designed to prevent persons associated with it from undertaking bribery.

The introduction of this new corporate criminal offence places a burden of proof on companies to show they have adequate procedures in place to prevent bribery. To avoid corporate liability for bribery, companies must make sure that they have strong, up-to-date and effective anti-bribery policies and systems.

The Act also provides for strict penalties for active and passive bribery by individuals as well as companies.

Bribing another person

A person is guilty of an offence if:

- They offer, promise or give financial or other advantage to another person with the intention of inducing someone to perform a relevant function or activity improperly, or to reward someone for the improper performance of such a function or activity.
- They offer, promise of give a financial or other advantage to another person, knowing or believing that the acceptance of the advantage would itself constitute the improper performance of a relevant function or activity.

It does not matter whether the person to whom the advantage is offered, promised or given is the same person as the person who is to perform, or has performed, the function or activity concerned.

Being bribed

A person is guilty of an offence if they request, agree to receive or accept a financial or other advantage intending that, in consequence, a relevant function or activity should be performed improperly, or as a reward for the improper performance of a relevant function or activity.

It does not matter whether the relevant function or activity is performed improperly by the person being bribed or by another at their request or with their assent or acquiescence, nor whether the bribe is requested, agreed or accepted directly or through a third party, nor whether the advantage is for the person requesting the bribe or another person.

It does not matter whether those involved know or believe that the performance of the function or activity is improper.

Bribing a foreign public official

A person who bribes a foreign public official is guilty of an offence if their intention is to obtain or retain business, or an advantage in the conduct of business.

Failure by an organisation to prevent bribery

A commercial organisation is guilty of an offence if a person associated with the organisation is guilty of bribery and the organisation does not have adequate procedures to prevent adequate procedures in place to prevent bribery.

Territorial reach

The Act has extra-territorial reach both for UK companies operating abroad and for overseas companies with a presence in the UK.

A company can commit an offence of failure to prevent bribery if an employee, subsidiary, agent or service provider bribes another person anywhere in the world to obtain or retain business or a business advantage. A foreign subsidiary of a UK company can cause the parent company to become liable when the subsidiary commits an act of bribery in the context of performing services for the UK parent.

The Act also has important implications for foreign companies that do business in the UK, as its territorial scope is extensive. The corporate offence of failure to prevent bribery in the course of business applies to any relevant commercial organisation defined as a body incorporated under the law of the United Kingdom and any overseas entity that carries on a business or part of a business in the United Kingdom. As a result, a foreign company that carries on any part of its business in the UK could be prosecuted for failure to prevent bribery even where the bribery takes place wholly outside the UK and the benefit or advantage to the company is intended to accrue outside the UK. The company's only statutory defence would be to prove the existence of adequate systems and controls.

Board performance evaluation and director appraisal

Good governance requires that the performance of the board be evaluated once a year. The board should undertake a formal and rigorous annual evaluation of its own performance and that of its committees and individual directors.

Evaluation of the board should consider the balance of skills, experience, independence and knowledge of the company on the board, its diversity, including gender, how the board works together as a unit and other factors relevant to its effectiveness.

A well conducted evaluation helps the board, committees and individual directors perform to their maximum capabilities.

- Assess the balance and currency of skills within the board
- Identify attributes required for any new appointments
- Review practice and process to improve efficiency and effectiveness
- Consider the effectiveness of the board's decision making processes
- Recognise the board's outputs and achievements

The evaluation process is a mechanism to improve board effectiveness, maximise strengths and tackle weaknesses, leading to an immediate improvement of performance throughout the organisation.

Individual evaluation should aim to demonstrate whether each director continues to contribute effectively and to demonstrate commitment to the role (including commitment of time for board and committee meetings and any other duties).

The non-executive directors led by the senior independent director, should be responsible for performance evaluation of the chairman, taking into account the views of executive directors.

The chairman should act on the results of the performance evaluation by recognising the strengths and addressing the weaknesses of the board and, where appropriate, proposing new members to be appointed or seeking the resignation of directors.

The board should state in the annual report how performance evaluation of the board and its committees and individual directors has been conducted.

A performance evaluation can play a key role in helping give the board: -

- Clarity of purpose that can be communicated throughout the organisation
- More productive board meetings that look forwards and outwards rather than inwards and backwards
- Faster and more effective decision-making, that can be translated onto the bottom line
- Better personal relationships and appreciation of individual roles, leading to a more collaborative approach within the board and with internal and external stakeholders
- Better succession planning, recruitment, induction and appraisal of directors

- Increased personal satisfaction with less stress

The UK Corporate Governance Code requires evaluation of boards of FTSE 350 companies to be externally facilitated at least every three years and for the external facilitator to be identified in the annual report with a statement as to whether they have any other connection with the company.

The New York Stock Exchange requires annual board evaluations, although companies retain great flexibility around what to assess and how, as well as how to apply the results.

Check out your behaviour now

Check out your behaviour and what you have learned against the corporate governance checklists in Chapter 16.

Find out more about director development and corporate governance at: www.corporatedirector.co.uk

5. Company finance

Share capital – equity

Ordinary shares

Ordinary shares are issued to the owners of a company. They have a nominal or 'face' value, typically of £1 or $1. The market value of a quoted company's shares bears no relationship to their nominal value, except that when ordinary shares are issued for cash, the issue price must be equal to or be more than the nominal value of the shares.

The authorised or nominal share capital is the amount of capital the company is registered with, and is listed in the Memorandum of Association. This is the total of the nominal amounts written on each share. To change the authorised share capital, a special resolution must be passed.

The issued share capital is the amount of the authorised share capital that has been issued. This may not be equal to the authorised share capital if the company has retained some shares. It represents the funding a company has received from its members.

The called-up share capital is the total amount that has been called up from shareholders. If shares do not have to be paid immediately, directors may choose when finance can be called from shareholders.

The paid-up share capital is the total amount that has been paid. The difference between called-up and paid-up share capital is the amount owing from shareholders, which is often zero. Any references to 'capital' in a company's accounts or business letters must refer to paid-up capital.

A rights issue provides a way of raising new share capital by means of an offer to existing shareholders, inviting them to subscribe cash for new shares in proportion to their existing holdings.

A scrip issue (also called a capitalisation issue or a bonus issue) is a form of secondary issue where a company's cash reserves are converted into new shares and given to existing shareholders at no charge, *pro rata* to their existing shareholdings. It is basically a bookkeeping exercise and the value of any shareholdings is unchanged by a scrip issue despite the increase in the number of shares held.

However, a scrip issue can have an impact on the share price for two reasons:

- A scrip issue is a gesture of confidence. The amount available to pay dividends is reduced – therefore it can be inferred that the management of the company is sure that the amount capitalised will not be needed to pay dividends.
- It can improve the liquidity of very high priced shares, if the old share price was so high as to make the trading of small blocks awkward.

Ordinary shares carry a right to vote, but have no fixed dividend. Dividends paid on ordinary shares are determined at the AGM and can only be paid if sufficient distributable profits are available. In addition, when a company is liquidated, if any money is left after all creditors have been paid and shares have been redeemed, then this is shared between ordinary shareholders.

Some companies create different classes of ordinary shares, *e.g.* 'A' and 'B' ordinary shares with different nominal values or voting rights. This can allow founders to attract more investment without having to give up control.

For example, the Murdoch family was able to control News Corporation whilst owning only 12% of the company. Seventy percent of the shares carried no voting power, but the Murdochs held almost 40% of the "B shares" that did carry a vote.

Preference shares

Preference shares do not normally carry a right to vote, but command a fixed percentage dividend before any dividend is paid to the ordinary shareholders. As with ordinary shares a preference dividend can only be paid if funds are available, although with 'cumulative' preference shares the right to an unpaid dividend is carried forward to later years. The arrears of dividend on cumulative preference shares must be paid before any dividend is paid to the ordinary shareholders.

Early stage investors

Angel investors are individuals and businesses that are interested in helping small businesses survive and grow by providing start-up or early-stage funding. In addition to providing convertible debt or equity finance, they bring their own expertise and knowledge to the running of the business.

Venture capitalists provide early-stage funding to companies with strong growth potential. In exchange for the high risk, they usually expect to get significant control over company decisions as well as a significant portion of the equity. Venture capitalists invest for capital growth and will expect sell their equity in three to seven years, either through an initial public offering (IPO) or through a merger or trade sale. The chose exit strategy will have implications for the future role of the original owners.

Loan stock

Loan stock is long-term debt capital raised by a company for which interest is paid, usually half yearly and at a fixed rate. Holders of loan stock are therefore long-term creditors of the company.

Loan stock has a nominal value, which is the debt owed by the company, and interest is paid at a stated "coupon yield" on this amount. Debentures are a form of loan stock, legally defined as the written acknowledgement of a debt incurred by a company, normally containing provisions about the payment of interest and the eventual repayment of capital.

Loan stock and debentures will often be secured by either a fixed charge on a specific asset or group of assets, typically land and buildings, or a floating charge on general assets of the company, such as stocks and debtors.

Internally generated cash

Retained earnings

Retaining profits, instead of paying them out in the form of dividends, offers a simple low-cost source of finance. Profit re-invested as retained earnings is profit that could have been paid as a dividend.

Working capital

Working capital is the cash available for day-to-day business. It is the difference between current assets (accounts receivable and inventory) and current liabilities (accounts payable).

Depending on the timing of receipts and payments, your customers and suppliers can be a source of cash, or a drain on your working capital. Sometimes it can be beneficial to negotiate payment terms in return for a discount for early of late payment.

Bank lending

Borrowings from banks are an important source of finance to companies.

Overdrafts provide flexible lending within a limit set by the bank and which is repayable on demand.

Bank loans provide short-, mid- or long-term financing, and they finance all asset needs, including working capital, equipment and real estate.

For smaller companies, banks are likely to require personal guarantees and even a secured interest on personal assets.

Leasing and factoring

Leasing fixed assets conserves cash for working capital, which is generally tougher to finance, especially for an unproven business.

Debt factoring involves taking over the business's debt collection. The factor is usually prepared to make an advance to the business of a maximum of 80 per cent of approved trade receivables. In addition to operating normal credit control procedures, a factor may offer to undertake credit investigations and to provide protection for approved credit sales. The charge made for the factoring service is based on total sales revenue, and is often 2 to 3 per cent of sales revenue. Any advances made to the business by the factor will attract a rate of interest similar to the rate charged on bank overdrafts.

Check out your behaviour now

Check out your behaviour and what you have learned against the corporate governance checklists in Chapter 16.

Find out more about director development and corporate governance at: www.corporatedirector.co.uk

6. Roles and Responsibilities of Directors

Role of the board of directors

The board's key purpose is to ensure the company's prosperity by collectively directing the company's affairs, whilst meeting the appropriate interests of its shareholders and stakeholders.

The board of directors is responsible for:

- Compliance
- Strategy

The objects of the company are defined in the Memorandum of Association and regulations are laid out in the Articles of Association.

According to the UK Institute of Directors, the tasks of the board are as follows:

Establish vision, mission and values

- Determine the company's vision and mission to guide and set the pace for its current operations and future development.
- Determine the values to be promoted throughout the company.
- Determine and review company goals.
- Determine company policies.

Set strategy and structure

- Review and evaluate present and future opportunities, threats and risks in the external environment and current and future strengths, weaknesses and risks relating to the company.
- Determine strategic options, select those to be pursued, and decide the means to implement and support them.
- Determine the business strategies and plans that underpin the corporate strategy.

- Ensure that the company's organisational structure and capability are appropriate for implementing the chosen strategies.

Delegate to management

- Delegate authority to management, and monitor and evaluate the implementation of policies, strategies and business plans.
- Determine monitoring criteria to be used by the board.
- Ensure that internal controls are effective.
- Communicate with senior management.

Exercise accountability to shareholders and be responsible to relevant stakeholders

- Ensure that communications both to and from shareholders and relevant stakeholders are effective.
- Understand and take into account the interests of shareholders and relevant stakeholders.
- Monitor relations with shareholders and relevant stakeholders by gathering and evaluation of appropriate information.
- Promote the goodwill and support of shareholders and relevant stakeholders.

Responsibilities of directors

Directors look after the affairs of the company, and are in a position of trust. This raises the possibility of them abusing their position in order to profit at the expense of their company, and, therefore, at the expense of the shareholders of the company.

Consequently, the law imposes a number of duties, burdens and responsibilities upon directors to prevent abuse. Much of company law can be seen as a balance between allowing directors to manage the company's business so as to make a profit, and preventing them from abusing this freedom.

Directors are responsible for ensuring that proper books of account are kept.

Even though a company is a separate legal person, there are circumstances in which a director can be required to help pay its debts. For example, directors of a company who try to 'trade out of difficulty' and fail may be found guilty of 'wrongful trading' and can be made personally liable. Directors are particularly vulnerable if they have acted in a way that benefits themselves.

- The directors must always exercise their powers for a 'proper purpose' – that is, in furtherance of the reason for which they were given those powers by the shareholders.
- Directors must act in good faith in what they honestly believe to be the best interests of the company, and not for any collateral purpose. This means that, particularly in the event of a conflict of interest between the company's interests and their own, the directors must always favour the company.
- Directors must act with due skill and care.
- Directors must consider the interests of employees of the company.

UK Companies Act 2006

The Companies Act, sections 170-178, sets out the legal responsibilities and general duties of company directors in the Statement of General Duties of Directors. The Act is based on established common law principles and case law, but also includes important reforms which affect all directors – executive or non-executive – in companies of every size.

Here is a summary of the main principles prepared by the Association of Chartered Certified Accountants.

The general duties mean a director must act in the interests of the company and not in the interests of any other parties - including shareholders. This applies even for 'one man' companies, which means a sole shareholder or director may not put their interests above that of the company.

Duty to act within the company's powers

In addition to the duties and responsibilities imposed on directors by the Act, every company will have its own set of rules known as its 'constitution'.

- Directors must follow the rules and restrictions contained in the constitution.
- They must use the powers designate to them by the shareholders for the benefit of the company.

Duty to promote the success of the company

The term 'success' is not defined in the Act because this may vary from company to company. In most cases, however, it is likely to mean sustainable profitability. The underlying principle here is that every director has a legal duty to try and act in such a way which, in their judgement, is most likely to bring 'success' to the company.

Duty to exercise independent judgement

This is self explanatory but the Act will not be breached if you exercise your duties in line with any prior agreement with the company or with the company's constitution.

Duty of skill, care and diligence

Every director must exercise reasonable care, skill and diligence in everything they do for the company. The duty is broken into two parts:

- As a director you must demonstrate the general knowledge and skill reasonably expected of a person carrying out the functions you carry out in relation to the company. Therefore, a managing director will be expected to have a knowledge of all areas of the business or to have engaged people who can help them; and
- As a director you must act in accordance with any specific general knowledge and skills you actually have. Therefore, a director who is a qualified accountant would be expected to show a greater general knowledge, skills and interest in relation to financial aspects of the company than another directors who was not so qualified.

Duty to avoid conflicts of interest

You must avoid any situations where you have any personal or outside interests which will potentially come into conflict with those of the company.

This duty even extends to former directors.

However, this duty is not infringed if:

- the situation cannot reasonably be regarded as likely to give rise to a conflict; or
- the matter has been authorised by the directors, as appropriate to the type of company (public companies must give the directors specific powers in their articles)

Duty not to accept benefits from third parties

A director of a company must not accept a benefit from a third party arising from them being a director; or from their actions as a director.

Any benefits that cannot reasonably be regarded as likely to give rise to a conflict of interest can be ignored.

This duty also applies to former directors.

Duty to declare an interest in a proposed transaction or arrangement

The Act states: "If a director of a company is in any way, directly or indirectly, interested in a proposed transaction or arrangement with the company he [she] must declare the nature and extent of that interest to the other directors."

The declaration of an interest can be either verbal or written but must comply with the requirements set out in the Act.

The Act also requires directors to consider a number of factors when making decisions, including the interests of the company's employees and the impact of the company's operations on the community and the environment. The duty only extends to considering the decisions' impact.

Appointment of directors

The ultimate control as to the composition of the board of directors rests with the shareholders, who can always appoint, and – more importantly, sometimes – dismiss a director. The shareholders can also fix the minimum and maximum number of directors. However, the board can usually appoint (but not dismiss) a director to this office as well. A director may be dismissed from office by a majority vote of the shareholders, provided that a special procedure is followed. The procedure is complex, and legal advice will always be required.

Non-executive directors

Legally speaking, there is no distinction between an executive and non-executive director. Yet there is inescapably a sense that the non-executive's role can be seen as balancing that of the executive director, so as to ensure the board as a whole functions effectively. Whereas the executive director has an intimate knowledge of the company, the non-executive director may be expected to have a wider perspective of the world at large.

Election of a chairman for the board

The company's articles of association usually provide for the election of a chairman of the board. They empower the directors to appoint one of their own number as chairman and to determine the period for which he is to hold office. If no chairman is elected, or the elected chairman is not present within five minutes of the time fixed for the meeting or is unwilling to preside, those directors in attendance may usually elect one of their number as chairman of the meeting.

Since the chairman's position is of great importance, it is vital that his election is clearly in accordance with any special procedure laid down by the articles and that it is unambiguously minuted; this is especially important to avoid disputes as to his period in office. Usually there is no special procedure for resignation. As for removal, articles usually empower the board to remove the chairman from office at any time. Proper and clear minutes are important in order to avoid disputes.

Role of the chairman

The chairman's role is pivotal to the operation of the board. He or she must coordinate the contributions of the non-executive directors to ensure that the executive team is subject to a sufficient degree of oversight.

As a general rule, the chief executive leads the management team and runs the company while the chairman leads the board. The chairman must be sufficiently informed, engaged and able to intervene when required, but must avoid becoming too involved with the day-to-day business of the company. Board dysfunction is likely to result when the distinct roles of the chief executive and chairman are not properly understood or respected.

The chairman's role includes managing the board's business and acting as its facilitator and guide. This can include:

- Determining board composition and organisation;
- Clarifying board and management responsibilities;
- Planning and managing board and board committee meetings;
- Developing the effectiveness of the board.

The company's articles might give the chairman a second, 'casting', vote to be used in the case of equality of votes. However, a chairman does not have a casting vote merely by virtue of his office.

What makes an outstanding chairman?

A study by INSEAD identified three characteristics of good chairmen: personal humility, listening, while challenging and supporting the board and the 'guts' to do what is right for the company.

The Directorbank Group surveyed 430 chairmen and directors to discover what makes an outstanding chairman. Here is what they found:

What makes them outstanding	What causes them to underperform
• Charismatic personality with gravitas • Good communicator and listener • Clear sense of direction • Strategic view – the big picture • Allows CEO to get on with their job • Good at governance; managing meetings • Public presence • Broad experience • Network of contacts • Business acumen; understands the business • Able to bring people together • A mentor and coach; offers support and advice • Able to gain shareholders' confidence • Able to get to the key issue quickly	• Too partisan, not impartial • Poor leadership • Too aloof and not involved • Arrogant, over-opinionated and domineering • Poor control of the board • Unable to make difficult decisions • Doesn't properly understand the business • Poor sector knowledge • Poor communicator

Shadow directors

In many circumstances, the law applies not only to a director, but to a 'shadow director'. A shadow director is "a person in accordance with whose directions or instructions the directors of a company are accustomed to act". Under this definition, it is possible that a director, or the whole board, of a holding company, and the holding company itself, could be treated as a shadow director of a subsidiary.

Professional advisers giving advice in their professional capacity are specifically excluded from the definition of a shadow director in the company's legislation.

Calling a directors' meeting

A director, or the secretary at the request of a director, may call a directors' meeting. A secretary may not call a meeting unless requested to do so by a director or the directors. Each director must be given reasonable notice of the meeting, stating its date, time and place. Commonly, seven days is given but what is 'reasonable' depends in the last resort on the circumstances.

Building a better board

Highly effective boards include a mix of directors with expertise and experience to fulfil their essential oversight roles. Having a board made up of the right people with the relevant skill sets is critical in today's competitive business environment.

A board must have the minimum skills required to adequately cover the unique issues, risks and challenges that the particular business faces and these skills must be up to date.

A high performing board needs:

- leaders
- visionaries or strategic thinkers
- practical people
- analytical people
- communicators who can deal with stakeholder groups

Not all directors will possess each necessary skill but the board as a whole must possess them, and each member of the board must be able to work with the group in a constructive way that ensures there is a rigorous debate whilst remaining a highly functional group.

Juliet de Baubigny, a senior partner at Kleiner Perkins Caufield & Byers has identified some practical tips for assembling a great board.

Know the company's vision. Where do you want the company to go? Define what you need the board to do to achieve those goals. Keep that in mind as you consider and define the attributes, skills, and experiences that you need of your board members.

Seek the right skills. Create a simple grid combining attributes that actually exist in the market. Draft a table with all the desired aspects of a "final" board. Fill in the table with prospective ideas for each director, ranking each in terms of depth or fit and whether that person can be recruited. Keep this list current, fresh, and ongoing, and make it an active item of discussion at board meetings.

Develop roles and responsibilities for members. As Jim Collins says, "Do you have the right people in the right seats on the bus?" It's never too early to have committees or key areas of responsibility. Do you have the best head of audit, compensation etc.? Who are the lead directors that you as CEO can rely on in each critical area?

Build a culture and invite debate. Foster a culture of open feedback and independence. You want different opinions and perspectives to help you consider alternatives. Consider the culture and interaction you want from your board: passionate and intense debate, or cerebral and deliberative? You want to recruit a board that pushes you, makes you uncomfortable and challenges conventional wisdom. At the same time, you want a board and not an operating committee – so setting boundaries is important.

Break through your comfort zone. Boards tend to reach for what's familiar and comfortable, which results in homogeneity. Knowing that, you should strive for diversity of opinion and not be afraid to go against the grain. Keeping that top of mind will help you be open-minded to alternatives you would not have considered in the first place.

Board building is an ongoing activity, a process of continuous improvement, which means boards must keep coming back to the same questions about purpose, resources, and effectiveness. The best mechanisms for doing that are annual self-assessments. According to a survey undertaken by Mercer Delta Consulting and reported in the *Harvard Business Review* (May 2004), conducting and acting on such assessments are among the top activities most likely to improve board performance overall.

Boards must decide how engaged they want to be in influencing management's decisions and the company's direction. Mercer Delta Consulting have identified five board types that fall along a continuum from least to most involved. They recommend that at the start of any board-building programme, the directors and the CEO should agree among themselves which of the following models best fits the company.

The Passive Board

This is the traditional model. The board's activity and participation are minimal and at the CEO's discretion. The board has limited accountability. Its main job is ratifying management's decisions.

The Certifying Board

This model emphasises credibility to shareholders and the importance of outside directors. The board certifies that the business is managed properly and that the CEO meets the board's requirements. It also oversees an orderly succession process.

The Engaged Board

In this model, the board serves as the CEO's partner. It provides insight, advice, and support on key decisions. It recognises its responsibility for overseeing CEO and company performance. The board conducts substantive discussions of key issues and actively defines its role and boundaries.

The Intervening Board

This model is common in a crisis. The board becomes deeply involved in making key decisions about the company and holds frequent, intense meetings.

The Operating Board

This is the deepest level of ongoing board involvement. The board makes key decisions that management then implements. This model is common in early-stage start-ups whose top executives may have specialised expertise but lack broad management experience.

Establishing an overarching level of engagement helps board directors set expectations and ground rules for their roles relative to senior managers' roles. But an engagement philosophy – like most expressions of general principle – does not apply equally to all spheres of activity. Boards, after all, potentially participate in dozens of distinct areas.

Balancing a board with personality and skills

Although the formal authority to elect directors lies with the shareholders, the power to nominate board members is the key to forming an effective board.

Building an effective board takes time and patience on the part of board members, and benefits from a professional approach to boardroom procedure.

The essential step in building a first class professional board is to relate it to the company's needs. Every board should have a rationale – that is there should be an essential logic behind its size, structure and specific membership.

The chairman has a particular responsibility in welding a group of capable individual into an effective board team. The chairman has to find a way to reach a consensus between diverging views on the company and its future. An atmosphere of open discussion should be encouraged. Perspectives and view points should be properly documented in the minutes, allowing dissenting voices to be recorded. There should also be a clear formulation of decisions, so that the decision-making process is followed by decisive action.

It is important to ensure that due care is taken over the choice of board members, and that board members have the necessary skills and competencies to fulfil their responsibilities. Executive directors will need to undertake specialised professional training if they are to effectively make the transition from operational manager (with a focus on one aspect of a firm's activities) to company director (where they must exercise oversight over the firm as a whole).

A board must gel as a team and, as a team, control management. Any behaviour gap – undue influence, reliance, dislike, dysfunction or even contempt – by one or more directors or managers, introduces information and oversight asymmetry that can lead to governance failure.

Good boards have competency, diversity and behaviour matrices and performance reviews that define and rate behaviours at the board table, have peer reviews and mentoring that develops and refines behaviours, and act on the results regardless of profile or tenure.

In the Hermes *Responsible Capitalism Survey*, 2014, over 85% of institutional investors identified having a range of diverse professional experiences at board level and an independent board as important corporate governance practices when looking to make an investment.

The Australian Institute of Directors believes that two main sets of criteria should be met in determining the competencies required in a director:

- Behavioural attributes that contribute to an effective group dynamic. Each board member needs to be able to work with the group in a constructive way that ensures there is rigorous debate whilst remaining a highly functioning group.
- A board must have the minimum skills required to adequately cover the unique issues, risks and challenges

that the particular business faces and these skills must be up to date.

Individual directors and the board overall must make efforts to ensure each member remains up to date in both skills and knowledge.

The board must make an effort to regularly measure and assess the contribution each board member makes and take steps to address any deficiencies that become apparent. It should regularly audit the skills required by the company and adapt or make changes to the board membership according to changing needs.

Evaluation of directors should be undertaken by the nominating committee and its independent advisor, not by management.

In their book *Board Composition and Corporate Performance* (2003), Keil and Nicholson describe a high performing board as having:

- Leaders
- Visionaries or strategic thinkers
- Practical people
- Analytical people
- Communicators who can deal with stakeholder groups.

Not all directors need to possess each necessary skill but the board as a whole must possess them.

Competencies for board members can be broken into job-related skills necessary to do their job and personal qualities:

Job-related competencies

- Strategic expertise – the ability to review the strategy through constructive questioning and suggestion.
- Accounting and finance – the ability to read and comprehend the company's accounts, financial material presented to the board, financial reporting requirements and some understanding of corporate finance.
- Legal – the board's responsibility involves overseeing compliance with numerous laws as well as understanding an individual director's legal duties and responsibilities.
- Managing risk – experience in managing areas of major risk to the organisation.
- Managing people and achieving change.
- Experience with financial markets.

- Industry knowledge – experience in similar organisations or industries.

Personal qualities

- An effective and persuasive communicator whose contribution is concise, objective and clear.
- Socially competent with a deft touch of humour.
- Independent of mind without prejudicing loyalty to colleagues and the board.
- A good listener who can focus on key issues and respond with sound advice.
- Democratic in balancing the interests of shareholders against the interests of others involved in the business.
- An achiever in his or her own particular chosen field.
- Constructive in expressing ideas as an individual when divorced from the structure and props of his or her own organisation (non-executive directors)
- Positive in making statements and proposals, and unwilling to acquiesce in silence.

Personality profiling

Personality profiling is a means of studying the dynamic structure of a team and matching individuals to roles and responsibilities.

Individual and team profile analysis is a systematic procedure designed to measure personal behavioural styles. Profiling helps individuals gain an understanding of their working style, how this impacts on their relationships with others in the business environment, and how they might develop to improve their effectiveness both as a person and as a professional. It enables them to further enhance their inter-personal skills, improving team performance and creating a more positive, productive cultural environment.

Although it is very useful for individuals to understand both how they operate and where best to target their talents, the real benefit is when a whole team can be profiled and then discuss how the team works together.

Profiling systems include DISC, Belbin Team Roles and Myers-Briggs Type Indicator. Brefi Group uses the Wealth Dynamics system.

Wealth Dynamics

Wealth dynamics is a very user-friendly profiling system that defines eight profiles in terms of the roles in which different individuals are most likely to be successful. This will identify strengths and weaknesses in the balance of the board, which, when related to the experience/knowledge/skills register, can be used in future recruitment.

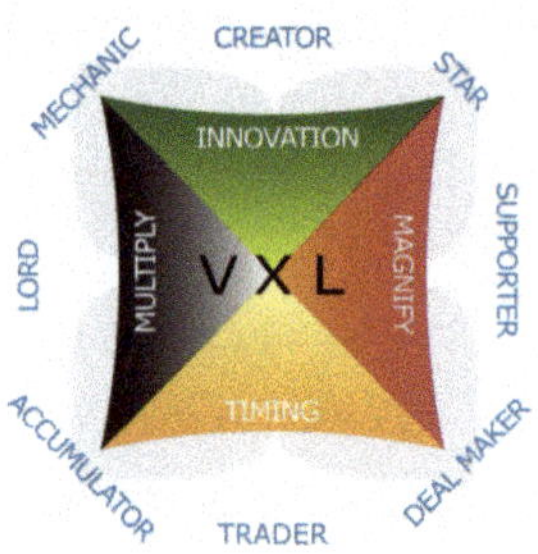

Wealth Dynamics is an on-line system that provides individual printed reports. However, it is desirable for both the individual and the team to receive an explanation of the system and personal feedback from a qualified consultant.

You can learn about Wealth Dynamics and obtain a personal profile at: www.knowyourprofile.com.

Building a board as the company grows

By Cara Cunningham, from *Red Herring*, October 30, 2000

Ideally a board of directors operates independently from a company, but oversees it with the company's best interests in mind.

Ideally, that is. In reality, many companies end up with much less because their chief executives don't know how to build their boards. Instead of carefully researching board candidates, they pick friends, yes-men, people they heard speak at conferences, or just about anyone who will offer them funding.

A better way to build a board is to plan it from the start, by establishing a board of advisers as soon as the company is founded. The advisers help entrepreneurs develop business plans and product strategies, but don't have any obligation to the company's shareholders. These advisers often evolve into board members.

When the founders seek their first round of venture capital, they should pay attention to the quality of the VCs who come with it.

Once founders accept the money, those VCs will likely be named to the board.

After closing on the first round of funding, a typical board has four or five members, including executives and VCs. More likely than not, the chief executive is also chairman. That may be a passable arrangement at first. But over time, a board should grow to have a majority of outside directors, who neither work for the company nor have a vested interest in it, according to CalPERS (California Public Employees' Retirement System), a major investor that sets and studies board governance guidelines.

also recommends that the CEO and chairman be different people; that way a CalPERS company avoids the conflict of having a CEO command the board that commands the CEO.

When adding board members, the board should take stock of what the company lacks, like industry contacts, operational experience, name recognition, or strategic planning, and then start filling in the holes.

"A lot of the time entrepreneurs are getting into a business where there's one aspect that they don't know well, so that's a great place to bring in a board member," says Warren Packard, managing director of Draper Fisher Jurvetson. General Electric chairman Jack Welch recently appointed golf buddy and Sun Microsystems CEO and chairman Scott McNealy to GE's board. Mr McNealy offers advice on GE's technology plans, and gets advice from Mr Welch on managing a big corporation.

Mr Packard also advises bringing in one outside board member to act as the CEO's coach. Ideally, the coach has been a CEO for years and can spend one-on-one time teaching the entrepreneur the ropes of the job.

Some board members aren't qualified to serve because they're too busy with other commitments. (VCs are notorious for this – some sit on more than 20 boards at a time.) CalPERS recommends that boards decide the maximum number of competing time commitments a member can have, and update those guidelines annually.

Appointing a director

Appointing directors who are able to make a positive contribution is one of the key elements of board effectiveness.

The nomination committee, usually led by the chairman, should be responsible for board recruitment. The process should be continuous and proactive, and should take into account the company's agreed strategic priorities. The aim should be to secure a board which achieves the right balance between challenge and teamwork, and fresh input and thinking, while maintaining a cohesive board.

The chairman's vision for achieving the optimal board composition will help the nomination committee review the skills required, identify gaps, develop transparent appointment criteria and inform succession planning.

It is important to consider a variety of personal attributes among board candidates, including: intellect, critical assessment and judgement, courage, openness, honesty and tact; and the ability to listen, forge relationships and develop trust. Diversity of psychological type, background and gender is important to ensure that a board is not composed solely of like-minded individuals.

Executive directors may be recruited from external sources, but companies should also develop internal talent and capability.

Given the importance of committees in many companies' decision-making structures, it will be important to recruit non-executives with the necessary skills and knowledge relating to the committees' subject matter, as well as the potential to assume the role of committee chairman.

Terms of engagement

If a prospective non-executive director decides to accept the offer of the appointment, terms of engagement should be agreed with the company (either the board as a whole or its nomination committee).

The terms that must be agreed are as follows:

- The initial period of tenure in office (normally three years);
- Time commitment: the company must indicate how much time the non-executive director is expected to commit to the company, and the non-executive director should make this commitment. This should be included in the formal letter of appointment. This is particularly important in the case of chairmanships;
- Remuneration: the annual remuneration of the non-executive director should be agreed. This may be a fixed annual fee. It is generally considered inappropriate for non-executive directors, including the chairman, to be remunerated on the basis of incentive schemes linked to company performance, because this could undermine their independence.

The terms of engagement should be set out in a formal letter of appointment. As well as including details of the role that the NED will be required to perform (including initial membership of board committees), the expected time commitment, the tenure and the remuneration, the letter of engagement should also:

- specify that the non-executive director should treat all information received as a director as confidential to the company;
- indicate the arrangements for induction;
- give details of directors' and officers' liability insurance that will be available;
- indicate the need for an annual performance review process for directors;
- state what company resources will be made available to the non-executive director.

Succession planning and recruitment

Appointing directors who are able to make a positive contribution is one of the key elements of board effectiveness. Directors will be more likely to make good decisions and maximise the opportunities for the company's success in the longer term if the right skill sets are present in the boardroom. This includes the appropriate range and balance of skills, experience, knowledge and independence. Non-executive directors should possess critical skills of value to the board and relevant to the challenges facing the company.

Given the importance of committees in many companies' decision-making structures, it will be important to recruit non-executives with the necessary technical skills and knowledge relating to the committees' subject matter, as well as the potential to assume the role of committee chairman.

For an organisation to plan for the replacement of key managers and directors from within, potential candidates must first be identified and prepared to take on those roles.

Succession planning is a means for an organisation to ensure its continued effective performance through leadership continuity. When recruiting new directors it is important to be clear what competencies, skills and experiences are needed on the board and which ones, if any, are missing. To assist in clarifying this information the board should ensure that there is an up-to-date director competency matrix. The process of developing the matrix should describe the competencies, skills, and experiences of the current directors and the key ones required for new directors.

The key steps in the competency matrix development process are likely to be as follows:

1. Assess what competencies the board *needs* given the challenges faced by the business and taking into account the strengths and weaknesses of the executive team. The roles and responsibilities of board and management are different but the capabilities of each need to be complementary. Consideration should also be given to weighting particular competencies.
2. Assess what competencies each *existing* director possesses. This is done by asking current board members to self assess themselves and their colleagues relative to the matrix. Those self assessments should be reviewed by, for example, the board chair or the nominating committee as some directors tend to be excessively modest while others overestimate themselves.
3. Evaluate the extent of any competency gaps resulting from a comparison between steps 1 and 2.
4. Define a 'recruitment specification' for the competencies a new director would need to bring to the board to fill defined competency gaps.

This allows potential internal candidates to be "groomed," trained, and mentored for the possibility of filling the leadership positions.

In order to prepare potential directors, the gap between what they are ready for now and what preparation they need to be ready for the job when it is available needs to be determined. This information can help determine what training, experience, and mentoring is needed.

Once the potential directors have been identified, a plan for each of them should be developed. Each potential director should be assigned a mentor; this mentor could be the person whom they might replace.

When the time comes for the position to be filled, there will be several people within the organisation from which to choose, all of whom have had the time to develop for the new role. At least one of them may be ready to meet the requirements.

For non-executive directors and external candidates for senior management roles the same approach should be taken to developing a recruitment specification. This will guide formal searches and form the basis for nomination committees to evaluate candidates. They must then conduct due diligence and closely scrutinise whether individual candidates possess the requisite skill set and qualities to serve on the board.

7. The non-executive director

Non-executive directors (NEDs) are members of the board of directors without executive responsibilities in the company.

They are appointed from outside the organisation for their independence, expertise and contacts to bring judgement and experience to the deliberations of the board that the executive directors on their own would lack. An NED will therefore attend board meetings and contribute to discussions and decision-making.

Non-executive directors are appointed to monitor executive activity and contribute to the development of strategy. This is a complex and demanding role that requires skills, experience, integrity and particular behaviours and personal attributes and it is the responsibility of the chairman to create accountability between the executives and non-executives.

In small companies they can contribute corporate expertise and provide a mentoring role. In larger companies an appointment can provide a training opportunity as a first experience on a board.

Non-executive directors need to be sound in judgement and to have an enquiring mind. They should question intelligently, debate constructively, challenge rigorously and decide dispassionately; and they should listen sensitively to the views of others, inside and outside the board.

A function of NEDs is to improve the quality of decision-making by the board by: bringing a range of skills and experience to the deliberations of the board; acting as a counterbalance, where necessary, to the influence of the chairman or CEO over board decision-making. They can make an important contribution to strategy by noticing blind spots and challenging executives to think laterally about options, alternatives and aspirations in a way that is nevertheless felt to be supportive. It is the combination of informed challenge and support that executives most desire and value in the contribution of non-executives.

The key to non-executive effectiveness lies not in strengthening either the control or strategic aspects of their role but in the strength and rigour of the process of accountability that they establish and maintain in their relationships with executives; accountability that spans issues of both their direction and control of the company.

Acting as an NED on the board of a young company that is dominated by the founder(s) and owners can require particularly sensitive soft skills of rapport building and communication, as well as decision making, vision and imagination. However, an NED with experience in larger or more established organisations can play a significant, if unacknowledged, role as a mentor in smaller ones.

To be effective, a non-executive director has to understand the company's business, but the experience and qualities required of an NED can be obtained from working in other industries or in other aspects of commercial and public life. NEDs might, therefore, include individuals who:

- are executive directors in other public companies;
- hold NED positions and chairmanship positions in other public companies;
- have professional qualifications (e.g. partners in firms of solicitors);
- have experience in government, as politicians or former senior civil servants.

The Higgs Report, 2003, looked at the role and effectiveness of NEDs, and many of the Higgs recommendations are now included in the UK Corporate Governance Code.

The Higgs *Suggestions for Good Practice* states that the role of a NED has several key elements, which non-executives are perhaps in a better position to provide than executives. These are:

- **Strategy:** NEDs should constructively challenge and help to develop proposals on strategy.
- **Performance:** NEDs should scrutinise the performance of executive management in achieving agreed goals and objectives, and monitor the reporting of performance.
- **Risk:** NEDs should satisfy themselves about the integrity of financial information and that the systems of internal controls and risk management are robust.
- **People:** NEDs are responsible for deciding the level of remuneration for executive directors, and should have a prime role in appointing directors (and removing them where necessary) and in succession planning.

These roles explain the requirements for audit, remuneration and nomination committees consisting of independent non-executive directors.

Much of their effectiveness depends on exercising influence rather than giving orders and requires the establishment of a spirit of partnership and mutual respect across the board. This requires the non-executive directors to build recognition by executives of their contribution in order to promote openness and trust. Only then can non-executives directors contribute effectively. The key to non-executive effectiveness lies as much in behaviours and relationships as in structures and processes.

Non-executive directors should be independent

The independence of a non-executive director could be challenged, for example, if the individual concerned:

- has a family connection with the CEO – a problem in some family-controlled public companies;
- until recently used to be an executive director in the company;
- until recently used to work for the company in a professional capacity (e.g. as its auditor or corporate lawyer);
- receives payments from the company in addition to their fees as an NED.

A key principle of good corporate governance is that there should be a sufficient number of independent NEDs on the board to create a suitable balance of power and prevent the dominance of the board by one individual or a small number of individuals.

A person cannot be independent if he or she personally stands to gain or otherwise benefit substantially from:

- income from the company, in addition to his or her fee as a NED;
- the company's reported profitability and movements in the company's share price.

These criteria of independence should be applied to a chairman as well as other non-executive directors.

Case study

The Kazhakstan mining company Kazakhmys attracted attention by becoming a listed UK company in October 2005 and a member of the FTSE 100. Although the company took steps to strengthen its corporate governance, its practices still fell short of normal UK listed company practice. Its chairman was not independent and there were doubts about the independence of the NEDs in view of the requirement of the Combined Code that independence means being free from relationships that affect, or could appear to affect, the judgement of the director.

One NED was a director of a company that had a large secured interest-free loan from Kazakhmys. Another NED received payment for services to the company in relation to its London listing. A third NED was vice chairman of investment banking at J P Morgan Cazenove, financial advisers to Kazakhmys.

A more general debate arose as a result of this case around whether corporate governance standards in the UK would come under threat as more foreign companies join the London market. Index-tracking funds would have to buy shares in these companies, even if their corporate governance regimes were not up to Corporate Governance Code standards.

Non-executive directors in small and mid-size quoted companies

According to a report of the triennial Quoted Companies Alliance/BDO Small and Mid-cap Sentiment Index for 2014, boards of small and mid-size quoted companies are relatively happy with the work that their non-executive directors do.

NEDs were seen as trusted members of their teams and clearly provide a unique viewpoint that is highly valued.

83 per cent of respondents felt that they got good value for money from their NEDs. They valued most their broader business experience, the fact that they provide checks and balances and the improvements in governance that they can bring to a company.

Non-executive directors in such companies work on average 14 hours per month and hold approximately three non-executive director roles. On average, they are paid £33,400 a year per role.

The report recommends that companies should do more to let their NEDs know what is expected of them. Demonstrating the valuable contribution of the NEDs on a board is an important way to inspire the confidence of private investors.

David Jones' recommendations for non-executive directors

David Jones was chief executive of the clothing retailer NEXT from 1988 until 2001 before becoming its chairman. In his business autobiography, *Next to Me*, he makes six recommendations for a new code of corporate governance with respect to non-executive directors:

- First, change the title of non-executive directors to 'independent directors', and call executive directors 'operating directors'. Independence of mind and a degree of distance from the internal politics and pressures of the day-to-day operations of the company are the key requirements. They are expected to be independent, so why not call them that?
- Second, make the senior independent director the deputy chairman, to ensure that his or her authority is clear to everyone, internally and externally.
- Third, ensure that there are an equal number of independent and operating directors. Balance is essential, and it is up to a skilled chairman to find consensus or exercise judgment if there is disagreement between the two groups.
- Fourth, insist that the independent directors spend at least three days of every month in the business. They must have a good knowledge of how the business operates in order to make a worthwhile contribution at board meetings. There is no excuse for not knowing what the executive directors are talking about or not understanding the board report. In addition, they must know the second tier of management to satisfy themselves that there is indeed a viable succession plan.
- Fifth, for the same reasons no-one – however, wise or well connected they may be – should be permitted to have more than three public independent directorships.
- Sixth, make it mandatory that the annual accounts of every public limited company should include a signed statement from each independent director confirming that they have had access to all the relevant information to enable them to do their jobs efficiently.

Check out your behaviour now

Check out your behaviour and what you have learned against the corporate governance checklists in Chapter 16.

Find out more about director development and corporate governance at: www.corporatedirector.co.uk

8. The Transition Phase

Transition from manager to director

During your career you will probably have taken on more responsibility and, at the same time, become more specialised. In effect you have moved from knowing very little about an awful lot to knowing an awful lot about a very little.

As you move up and up in your career you will become more expert in a narrower field, or focus only on the interests of a single department. Suddenly you become a director and everything is different, you need to show equal responsibility for all departments and to monitor a very wide and general environment, both inside the organisation and externally, changing your reading and viewing habits and acting as an ambassador for the company.

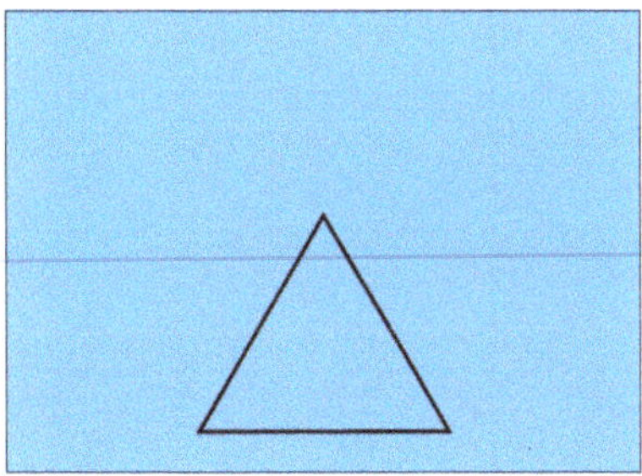

Context as head of department

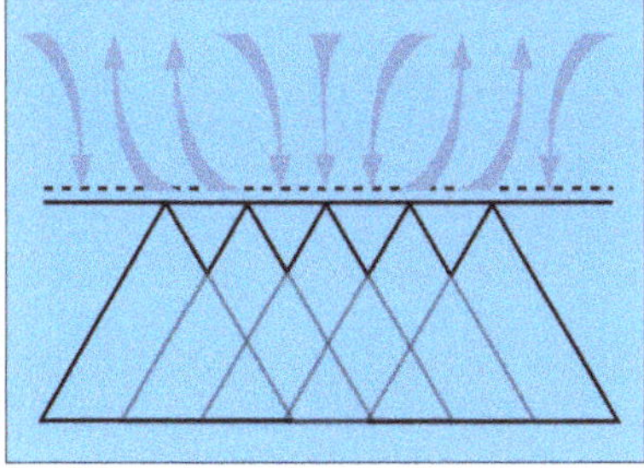

Context as board director

In addition, you will need to renegotiate your relationships with your colleagues as you take on a new status and identity.

Here are some of the issues you should consider:

- What are the challenges of the new role?
- What do your old colleagues expect of you now?
- How do you handle the change of status and relationships?
- What do your new board room colleagues expect of you?
- What do customers, suppliers and other stakeholders now expect?
- How do you handle dual responsibilities as head of department and board member?
- What practical steps should you take to improve your awareness, develop new skills, establish yourself in your new role?

One of your first steps should be to discuss these with your chairman and ensure that you have a full understanding of what is expected of you.

A promotion to a senior level such as director or partner brings with it new legal responsibilities, and the importance of understanding these should not be ignored. However, there are other, more subtle, things to consider.

If you are appointed from within, there needs to be a change of identity as well as of role. It is better if this is managed, rather than gradually evolving. If you are appointed from outside (a non-executive directorship is an important stage of many successful people's career development) there are additional issues of relationship building and access to information.

There should be a formal induction process for all new appointments, with a similar structure to the induction for any new role, but with particular attention paid to managing the change in relationships.

It is surprising how many directors continue to think like managers, even after two years on the board.

Here are five areas new directors should consider, even if there is no formal induction process.

- Have you discussed your new role with your chairman? Are you both clear about your role and responsibilities? Do you understand the culture and operating procedures of the board?

- What does it mean to you to be a director? How do you perceive other directors? Are you comfortable with your new identity?
- Have you discussed your new role with your staff and colleagues? What are their expectations of you now?
- How should you change the way that you trawl for information? What radio, television, newspapers and magazines should you access? What sorts of things should you notice?
- How and where should you network and how should you represent your organisation? Have you defined your new public identity and are you comfortable with it?

Induction and the first three months

The objective of induction is to provide a new director with the information he or she will need to become as effective as possible in their role within the shortest practicable time. Induction should include:

- Building an understanding of the nature of the company, its business and the markets in which it operates.
- Building a link with the company's people.
- Building an understanding of the company's main relationships.

All directors should receive induction on joining the board to obtain appropriate knowledge of the company and gain access to its operations and staff. The chairman should ensure that new directors receive a full, formal and tailored induction on joining the board.

The UK Institute of Chartered Secretaries and Administrators recommends that a new director should expect to make himself/herself available for an additional 10 days for the induction process. As part of this, directors should avail themselves of opportunities to meet major shareholders.

The company secretary is responsible for facilitating the induction programme under the direction of the chairman. One option is to partner a new non-executive director with a particular executive director to hasten an understanding of a particular part of the business.

Where the director will be joining a committee, he or she should be provided with copies of the committee minutes from the preceding 12 months.

Here is a checklist of issues to be addressed:

- Board and committee structure and terms of reference
- Biographical and contact details of all directors of the company, the company secretary and other key executives
- Board meetings, recent minutes, dates, procedures, and training in the use of systems and technology
- Boardroom behaviours, culture and values, codes of conduct/ethics
- Articles of association/constitution
- Board procedures and confidentiality
- Board appraisal and development programme
- Current issues
- The nature of the company, its business and its markets
- Meetings with senior management, visits to company sites, details of employee committees or surveys
- Information about main stakeholders

Establishing an individual job description

If this is the first time that you have acted as a director, a job description will draw attention to your duties under company law.

However, it is likely that you have been appointed for some specific purposes. If you are an executive director this will probably relate to your existing responsibilities. As a non-executive director, it is more important to understand what is expected of you and whether the chairman expects you to fulfil a specific responsibility. For example, you might be a lawyer but the chairman expects you to provide expert opinion on a part of the law for which you would need some additional study or training.

Here are the seven general statutory duties of a director as set out in the UK Companies Act 2006:

- To comply with the company's constitution and decisions made under the constitution and to exercise its powers only for the reasons for which they were given.
- To act in a way the director considers (in good faith) is most likely to promote the success of the company for the benefit of its members as a whole. In performing this duty, a director must have regard to all relevant matters, but the following are specifically identified in legislation:
    - o the likely consequences of any decision in the long term;
    - o the interests of the company's employees;

- the need to foster the company's business relationships with suppliers, customers and others; the impact of the company's operations on the community and the environment;
- the desirability of the company maintaining a reputation for high standard business conduct; and the need to act fairly as between members of the company.

- To exercise independent judgment, that is, not to subordinate the director's power to the will of others.
- To exercise reasonable care, skill and diligence.
- To avoid conflicts (or possible conflicts) between the interests of the director and those of the company.
- Not to accept benefits from third parties by reason of being a director or doing anything as director.
- To declare any interest in a proposed transaction or arrangement.

In addition to these duties, a director has duties:

- to consider or act in the interests of creditors (particularly in times of threatened insolvency)
- to maintain confidentiality of the company's affairs.

Check out your behaviour now

Check out your behaviour and what you have learned against the corporate governance checklists in Chapter 16.

Find out more about director development and corporate governance at: www.corporatedirector.co.uk

9. Practical Challenges

Obtaining information

All directors must ensure that, as individuals, they know what is going on and that they have adequate knowledge to make a contribution to board level discussions consistent with their own levels of expertise. Shareholders and courts are not sympathetic to directors, both executive and non-executive, who have not known enough about company matters.

Outside directors and the chairman should have access to the same information, and information systems, as the executive directors. However, directors have many sources of information in addition to board papers.

The secret to improving director-level information and understanding is not producing more reports or providing more data for directors. It is in providing opportunities for directors to be better informed, better able to direct the company, supervise executive management and be accountable for performance.

Knowledge and awareness can be developed from a wide range of sources. It is a director's responsibility to develop sensitivity and awareness to sources and subjects.

Formal and official information sources

Regular board papers:

- results by division and company
- monthly and annual accounts
- funds flow statement
- order book data
- project status etc.

Reports given in meetings

Official correspondence

Ad hoc reports and presentations

- special studies
- consultants' reports

- proposals for investment and acquisitions

Economic reports

- market reports
- research studies

Informal and unofficial information sources

Visits and presentations

Questioning in meetings

Contacts within the company

- face-to-face talks
- telephone
- email

Off-the-record comments

Grapevine discussion

Casual reading, radio, TV

Internet, Google, YouTube etc

Contacts outside the company

Conferences and networking events

Unofficial probing and questions

Processing information

Directors are not appointed to receive and approve information provided by the management. Their role is to process it intelligently and professionally.

Understanding issues

It might seem obvious that you should understand the information and issues that you are presented with. But it is easy to accept information at face value and to trust in others' expertise.

The quality of your contribution will be a function of the quality of your questions. Particularly when first appointed, be prepared to ask naïve questions and to keep on asking until you are confident that you have understood.

Where appropriate, take the time and trouble to ask for explanations or additional training outside board meetings. You have a legal right to professional advice and managers should be willing to help you.

Remember, as a director you are responsible for every decision taken at board level.

Group think

A characteristic of successful boards is the capacity to challenge one another's assumptions and beliefs. Respect and trust do not imply endless affability or absence of disagreement. Rather, they imply bonds among board members that are strong enough to withstand clashing viewpoints and challenging questions.

Directors are, almost without exception, intelligent, accomplished, and comfortable with power. But if you put them into a group that discourages dissent, they nearly always start to conform, and the ones that don't often decide to leave.

Frequently, head hunters looking for potential directors will ask, "Is this fellow a team player?" which is code for "Is this person compliant, or does he make trouble?" However, even a single dissenter can make a huge difference on a board.

Bernie Marcus, chairman of US retailer Home Depot, has been reported as saying, "I often say, 'I don't think you want me on your board. Because I am contentious. I ask a lot of questions and if I don't get the answers, I won't sit down.' That's the kind of board member that I want on my board . . . because our company needs help. We think we're bright, but we're not the smartest people in the world."

Sometimes an issue might seem straightforward, with everybody in agreement. This is a time to be cautious and, as a matter of course, to challenge the received opinion. Boards should make it standard practice to reconsider near unanimous decisions before going ahead.

This is particularly important for a major decision, such as an investment or acquisition in which there might already have been considerable investment of time and resources. Don't allow the board to be carried away by momentum.

Wilful blindness

In the 2006 case of the US Government vs. Enron, the presiding judge instructed the jurors to take account of the concept of 'wilful blindness' as they reached their verdict about whether the chief executives of the disgraced energy corporation were guilty. It was not enough for the defendants to say that they did not know what was going on; that they had not seen anything. If they failed to observe the corruption which was unfolding before their very eyes, not knowing was no defence. The guilty verdict sent shivers down the spine of the corporate world.

Group think and wilful blindness are psychological states that threaten any group tempted to think 'inside the box'. NEDs, in particular, should be constantly alert to these comfortable conditions.

Recording dissent

There might be times when you don't agree with a board decision. Although you will be bound by collective responsibility to support it, you should insist that your disagreement is recorded in the minutes.

Ensuring key issues are recorded

Although companies are protected by limited liability, directors are not. Apart from financial matters, directors are liable if the company fails to implement proper processes covering:

- Health and safety
- Employment law
- Control and disposal of hazardous waste

Your defence is to be able to prove that the board approved, implemented and monitored appropriate systems and processes.

Make sure that important issues are regularly considered and that decisions are recorded.

Conflicts of interest

In a company you may have several roles – as well as acting as a director, you might also own shares, lend the company money and guarantee loans, be a supplier or customer, or other significant stakeholder. Directors of more than one company should pay particular attention to the potential for conflicts of interest.

When there is a conflict of interests between various roles, the courts will usually support a director if they can show they have acted honestly, reasonably and transparently.

Where there is potential for a conflict of interest, directors must make a declaration of interest and will not be allowed to vote on such a matter.

Directors must not divert business opportunities to themselves that ought to be available to the whole company, nor should they benefit from a third party by reason of their being a director, or by doing or not doing something.

Directors must be extremely careful if they want to take advantage of an opportunity for private profit in an area of activity similar to that of the company – even if the company has rejected the particular proposition. If a director profits personally from his or her position, even if the company itself hasn't suffered because of their action, a court can order him or her to pass any profits made to the company.

Time commitment

To be able to fulfil the duties of a director, fully understanding issues and contributing productively, a director needs to commit sufficient time.

Obvious factors to consider include the number of board meetings held each year, the board committees on which a potential director might be expected to serve and the nature and amount of preparatory materials a company generally sends its directors prior to a meeting.

Many companies require a time commitment of 150 to 200 hours a year. However, in most cases, an individual will be required to allocate additional time to their board responsibilities, and the following activities will add to the amount of time a non-executive director must devote to a board:

- Becoming familiar with the specific industry in which a company operates, and with the business of the company in general
- Serving on committees of the board, especially serving on an audit committee

The average board commitment for a listed company has been quoted as 300 hours per year, with other estimates varying between 15 and 30 days.

Check out your behaviour now

Check out your behaviour and what you have learned against the corporate governance checklists in Chapter 16.

Find out more about director development and corporate governance at: www.corporatedirector.co.uk

10. Behaviours

Effective board practices

Unfortunately, many boards spend too much time on compliance and procedural matters and not enough high-quality time on other important issues, including CEO assessment, the succession process, strategy, development of leadership talent, and understanding the company's changing environment.

An excellent practice for getting the best return on a board's time is to adopt a 12-month agenda that specifies how much time each such issue will get in the coming year's meetings.

The agenda of the next meeting can be the last item to be discussed and agreed at the end of each board meeting.

The managing director/CEO should brief the board at least several times a year on the changing environment.

Proper preparation

Proper preparation is more than reading the board papers beforehand. Firstly, it is ensuring that you get the right information in an accessible format in time for you to study it. Then, of course, it is setting aside sufficient time in advance.

Best practice requires that information is provided sufficiently in advance of meetings to enable thorough consideration of the issues facing the board and that it is sufficient, accurate, clear and timely. You should insist on this.

In addition, according to the Higgs Report, you should continuously refresh your knowledge and skills and make sure that you are up to date with the latest developments in areas such as corporate governance and financial reporting, the industry and market conditions.

Preparation includes the time that you spend reading, watching and listening to the media, time spent networking and time spent visiting employees and the company's facilities. Make sure that as part of your directorship you allocate time for these activities, and don't take the easy path and assume that your duties are restricted to board meetings.

Asking naïve questions

According to Higgs, the effective non-executive director questions intelligently, debates constructively, challenges rigorously and decides dispassionately.

Particularly when you first join a board, you might not want to ask naïve or apparently stupid questions, but those questions are often the best way to spark a creative insight into problem solving and to challenge group think. Initially, this might require letting go of your ego, but you can refine it into an art – and maybe build yourself a reputation.

Assertiveness – being prepared to challenge

The core of all this, of course, is having the courage to challenge. It helps if you have previously discussed your role with the chairman and confirmed the importance and acceptability of challenge. If intelligent challenge is not welcomed then you should certainly consider your position.

Personal training and career development

The UK Financial Reporting Council's report "Guidance on Board Effectiveness" (2011) recommends that non-executive directors should devote time to developing and refreshing their knowledge and skills, including those of communication, to ensure that they continue to make a positive contribution to the board.

According to the UK Corporate Governance Code, the company should provide the necessary resources for developing and updating its directors' knowledge and capabilities. The chairman should regularly review and agree with each director their training and development needs and there should be an individual evaluation of each director to show whether they are continuing to contribute effectively. Such appraisals can be the basis for agreeing a personal development plan.

Quick check – board performance

Try these two quick checks on the performance of your board and of individual directors. They are based on the Institute of Directors publication *Good Practice for Directors – Standards for the Board*.

- We define and review the role and responsibilities of each individual director and how these contribute to the effectiveness of the board.

- Board members are effectively briefed in time to prepare for meetings.

- We regularly review the quality of the board's decisions, advice and its actions.

- The company's organisation structure and capability is appropriate for implementing its chosen strategies.

- Company objectives are consistent with the mission, values and needs of stakeholders, and form the basis of company strategy.

- The vision and mission are championed by the entire board throughout the organisation.

- The vision and mission are monitored and reviewed regularly

- Company objectives are Specific, Measurable, Achievable, Realistic and Time-bound.

- The board regularly reviews the company's Strengths, Weaknesses, Opportunities and Threats.

- The organisation's culture encourages continuous change and questioning of convention.

- The board clearly delegates authority to management and regularly reviews management's effectiveness.

- All staff, including me, receive a personal development review at least annually.

Quick check - director performance

- Directors rise above the immediate problem or situation and see the wider issue and implications.
- Directors are aware of the organisation's strengths and weaknesses and of the impact of the board's decisions upon them.
- Directors generate and recognise imaginative solutions and innovations.
- Directors show a readiness to take decisions, make judgements, take action and make commitments.
- Directors insist that sufficiently detailed and reliable information is taken account of, and reported as necessary.
- Directors probe the facts, challenge assumptions, identify the advantages and disadvantages of proposals, provide counter arguments, and ensure discussions are penetrating.
- Directors listen compassionately, intently and carefully; key points are recalled and taken into account.
- Directors are frank and open in their communications. They are willing to admit errors and shortcomings.
- Directors are able to persuade others to give their agreement and commitment; in face of conflict, they use personal influence to achieve compromise and agreement.
- Directors adopt a flexible (but not compliant) style when interacting with others. They take others' views into account and are prepared to change position when appropriate.

11. Effective meetings

Board meetings

Board meeting dates should be agreed in advance and 'fixed in stone' as far as possible. Frequent date changes can lead to poor attendance by non-executives.

The chairman should ensure that board meetings are run efficiently and should consider developing board guidelines with respect to meeting procedures and agenda setting. A typical structure for board meetings is as follows:

- An agenda should be prepared by the chairman
- The agenda and supporting papers should be circulated in advance of the meeting, allowing directors sufficient time to prepare
- Written minutes of board meetings should be taken. All decisions should be recorded, including dissenting opinions, along with assigned tasks and timescales. The minutes should also give an overview of the main topics discussed at the meeting
- Board meetings should monitor progress against approved plans and budgets, and ensure full coverage of matters reserved for the board

Clear and comprehensive minutes are an important safeguard for directors, who should take personal responsibility for ensuring that justifications and dissents are properly recorded.

Board members require relevant information on a timely basis in order to support their decision-making. However, a principal concern of many boards is not to increase the quantity of the information that they receive. Rather, it is to increase the quality. Information needs to be summarised and formatted in a manner that makes it accessible and useful for directors.

It is the board's responsibility to decide what information it wants and it should be constantly vigilant for 'information creep' and regularly review its relevance, comprehensibility and intelligibility. It should be part of the annual evaluation of the board's performance to examine whether the information provided to the board meets directors' expectations and requirements.

Meetings checklist

Timing and frequency

- Does the frequency of board meetings match the needs for strategy, monitoring and compliance?
- Are dates booked well in advance and do they relate to production of information, budget approval, annual general meeting and filing of statutory returns?

Agenda

- What is the purpose of the meeting? What is to be achieved?
- Who initiates the items on the agenda?
- Are some vital matters being ignored?
- Will the order of the items allow appropriate discussion? Will they hold interest and attention?
- Is an item of Any Other Business being used as an excuse for introducing matters unheralded, without prior documentation and with inadequate discussion?

Who should attend?

- Members
- Observers
- Providers of information

When?

- When will be convenient?
- Has there been enough notice?
- How long will the meeting last?
- Does the chairman insist on reasonable preparation time, or are too many reports tabled at the meeting?
- Would prior briefing for some directors be helpful?

How?

- Is a quorum required? If so, how many?
- What style of meeting? AGM, board meetings, committee meetings and corporate retreats will require different levels of structure and formality.
- Is there a recognised structure?

- Is this appropriate? Boards seldom take decisions by voting, rather reaching consensus by discussion, negotiation and compromise.

Where?

- Is the location appropriate for a board meeting, conducive to discussion and suitably equipped for presentations if required. Or is there a case to take the board to another part of the organisation, or to an outside location, an off-site corporate retreat – perhaps combining the meeting with a conference or visit?

What?

- What preparation is necessary?
- Is the prior paperwork adequate?

Minutes

- Are the minutes well written, noting the key issues, the decisions and the responsibilities for action?

Agendas

The agenda declares the structure and content of a meeting and provides the basis for setting expectations and guiding preparation.

During the meeting it helps with the allocation of time. It is very helpful if it differentiates items according to whether they are there for decision, discussion or information.

Here is a suggestion for a standard agenda:

Date/time

Location	**Estimated time**
Meeting opening	
Apologies	
Declarations of interest	
Approval of agenda	
Minutes and matters arising	
Matters for decision	
Major decisions	
Routine decisions	
Matters for discussion	
CEO's report	
CFO's report	
Advance discussion concerning strategic decision	
Committee minutes	
Other matters	
Chairman's update	
Presentations from management	
Matters for noting	
Major correspondence	
Calendar events	
Meeting finalisation	
Review actions to be taken	
Meeting evaluation	
Next meeting agenda	
Meeting closes	

Minutes

The minutes are an important record; they ensure that everyone understands what has been agreed, they confirm actions and they are the evidence for any future enquiry.

A director, usually the secretary, should keep a record of what went on at the meeting, including the results of votes, records of resolutions, and summaries of proposed ideas. The minutes need not contain any specialised language, but should accurately reflect what was said and done at the meeting. Items to include in the minutes are:

- the time, location, and members present at the meeting
- any pertinent company issues raised and a summary of some of the key issues raised in response to that issue
- the results of any votes conducted, including who voted for or against
- any other important information about what happened at the meeting.

A good rule of thumb is to include all information that a director who could not attend the meeting would need to know. Minutes should be filed with all other important company documents.

Meeting skills

Chairmanship

Chairing a meeting means ensuring that a meeting achieves its aims. The meeting should have been called for a specific purpose and all discussion at the meeting must be steered to this end. This may sound simple in theory but in practice it is a very demanding task.

Effective chairing is important because it can:

- Provide clear leadership and direction, ensuring that discussions are based on an agreed agenda and adhering to established ground rules, standing orders or protocols for how the business should be conducted.
- Ensure that debates are focused and balanced, involving discussion from all of those who wish to articulate a view, particularly where conflicting viewpoints are being expressed.
- Enable decisions to be reached, allowing participants to agree on the way forward and any further action that needs to be taken.

- Contribute to group or team working, allowing people to build rapport and contribute to group/committee discussions.
- Save time and energy, allowing information, views and evidence to be gathered in an efficient and timely manner

Chairmanship skills include:

- Impartiality
- Assertiveness
- Ability to stay on course
- Summarising

A good chairperson will:	A poor chairperson will:
Make all members feel valued	Be the person who talks most at the meetings
Strive for consensus, using his/her casting vote sparingly	Make all the decisions
Listen to others	Allow one or two people to dominate meetings
Encourage new faces onto committee	Cut people out of discussions
Plan for the future	Allow meetings to become unproductive
Make new members feel welcome	Make people feel foolish or useless
Allow others to take responsibility	Force people to contribute to discussions
Keep calm	Lose his/her temper
Know when to stand down	Stay too long

Four styles of chairman

In a study of chairmen and chief executives, the London based head hunters CCG identified four distinct, preferred styles of chairmanship:

- **The facilitator** chairman is hands-off, working with and through a chief executive. He or she has warm and open personal relationships with all board members. Their style is trusting, supportive, sensitive, aware and purposeful. There is a balance between head and heart, between deliberately standing back to see the wider prospective and involvement with people, issues and vision. This style was most popular, favoured by 32 per cent of respondents.

- **The thinker** works through a chief executive but has no doubt about their own power and is likely to get their way on the business issues. They can be a formidable combination with a chief executive, provided both agree on fundamentals. Although they are trusted, relationships will be more distant and based on respect, with a recognition of private agendas. Their penetrating understanding of the issues and the people is likely to be accompanied by strongly held (but not always disclosed) views. Favoured by 25 per cent.
- **The drinker** is likely to dominate by force of personality. There is a variety in the importance, closeness and style of their relationships, which are not always consistent but are not difficult to read. There is less emphasis on sophisticated analysis, or on the communication of a vision, and more on strategy, action and results. They require total loyalty and commitment, both to themselves and the company. They are unquestionably the boss; anyone carrying the title of chief executive will be at best a number two or a chief operating officer. Favoured by 23 per cent of respondents, though not much liked by chief executives.
- **The integrator** is talented at winning both hearts and minds. They are intellectually brilliant, with a flair for communication and relationships. Their style is open, trusting empathic and empowering. They have strong strategic and analytical skills, are able to see the big picture and are immersed in the business. They are more interested in the strategy than operations and would work best sharing leadership with a chief executive who complements their qualities. Preferred by 20 per cent or respondents, but most popular among non-executive directors.

Decision making

Well-informed and high-quality decision making is a critical requirement for a board to be effective and does not happen by accident. Flawed decisions can be made with the best of intentions, with competent individuals believing passionately that they are making a sound judgement, when they are not. Many of the factors which lead to poor decision making are predictable and preventable. Boards can minimise the risk of poor decisions by investing time in the design of their decision-making policies and processes, including the contribution of committees.

Most complex decisions depend on judgement, but the judgement of even the most well intentioned and experienced leaders can, in certain circumstances, be distorted. Some factors known to distort judgement in decision making are conflicts of interest, emotional attachments and inappropriate reliance on previous experience and previous decisions.

Boards can benefit from reviewing past decisions, particularly ones with poor outcomes. A review should not focus just on the merits of a decision but also on the decision-making process.

Check out your behaviour now

Check out your behaviour and what you have learned against the corporate governance checklists in Chapter 16.

Find out more about director development and corporate governance at: www.corporatedirector.co.uk

12. Performance Measures

Monitoring performance

It is management's responsibility, not the board's, to implement strategy.

However, it is important to ensure that business strategies and plans for different parts of the organisation are consistent with corporate strategy – and that they are implemented and the results monitored.

Although, on the face of it, the board's main role is to direct, in practice, monitoring is even more important.

When the Americans launched rockets to the moon, they were rarely on the exact correct course. NASA in Houston was continuously monitoring the direction and applying course corrections.

The board needs to be in a similar position – receiving enough information to enable it to know when to apply a course correction. The challenge is to communicate direction and to monitor key information (metrics) in order to maintain an effective but light touch.

This is a particular challenge for non-executive directors; to judge how much information they need in order to discharge their responsibilities without interfering.

An initial focus on business objectives enables definition of appropriate metrics – those that are meaningful to stakeholders and to the business. Effective metrics measure results in terms of defining action and improvement, rather than merely monitoring performance.

By selecting a few key metrics to begin with, organisations can secure initial successes and add more strategic elements and complexity. At board level about six high-level metrics should suffice.

It is helpful if information can be delivered in a user-friendly manner – not in complicated computer print-outs or spreadsheets. There are two processes that can help here.

Balanced Business Scorecard

The balanced business scorecard is a management system that is used to align business activities to the vision and strategy of the organisation, improve internal and external communications, and monitor organisation performance against strategic goals. It provides the key business drivers and criteria to motivate managers to develop and apply processes that will contribute to future success – rather than dwelling on historic performance.

The traditional means of measuring success through financial performance focuses on achievement to date. It is backward looking and can be counter productive in terms of securing a successful financial future.

By requiring four perspectives, the business scorecard provides a richer more holistic view of the organisation and balances financial success with processes that will generate success in the future.

The financial perspective is retained and 'balance' is achieved by introducing a customer perspective, an internal perspective and a learning and growth perspective. In addition, it introduces objectives and measures, identifying both critical success factors and critical measurements.

The four perspectives generally used are shown below. However, the model can be used with any selection of perspectives appropriate to a particular exercise.

Financial perspective	Customer perspective	Internal business processes	Learning and growth
To succeed financially, how should we appear to our shareholders?	To achieve our vision, how should we appear to our customers?	What business processes must we excel at?	How will we sustain our ability to change and improve?
• Objectives • Measures • Targets • Initiatives	• Objectives • Measures • Targets • Initiatives	• Objectives • Measures • Targets • Initiatives	• Objectives • Measures • Targets • Initiatives
What are the critical success factors?			
What are the critical success measures?			

Performance Dashboard

A performance dashboard is a performance management system that translates the organisation's strategy into objectives, metrics, initiatives and tasks customised to each group and individual in the organisation.

A performance dashboard lets business people:

- Monitor critical business processes and activities using metrics of business performance that trigger alerts when potential problems arise.
- Analyse the root cause of problems by exploring relevant and timely information from multiple perspectives and at various levels of detail.
- Manage people and processes to improve decisions, optimise performance and steer the organisation in the right direction.

Dashboards can be designed and developed to address a wide range of objectives, from monitoring the viability of a global organisation's business strategy, to keeping a check on a department's ability to achieve service-level targets.

At its simplest, a dashboard can simply be a set of visual display mechanisms that deliver performance information in a user-friendly way. However, a performance dashboard can also be a full-fledged business information system that is built on a business intelligence and data integration infrastructure that knits together the data, applications, and rules that drive what users see.

Properly designed and implemented performance dashboards will deliver the right information to the right users at the right time to optimise decisions, enhance efficiency and accelerate bottom-line results.

Internal controls

Most major corporate scandals have been the result of directors being unaware of the true financial position of the organisation for which they are responsible.

Every organisation should have a robust system of financial control. The organisation's auditors should be encouraged to review the controls in the business and report to the directors on their findings.

A company's system of internal control has a key role in the management of risks that are significant to the fulfilment of its business objectives. A sound system of internal control contributes to safeguarding the shareholder's investment and the company's assets.

Internal control encompass the policies, processes, tasks, behaviours and other aspects of a company that, taken together:

- facilitate its effective and efficient operation by enabling it to respond appropriately to significant business, operational, financial, compliance and other risks to achieving the company's objectives. This includes safeguarding of assets from inappropriate use or from loss and fraud and ensuring that liabilities are identified and managed;
- help ensure the quality of internal and external reporting. This requires the maintenance of proper records and processes that generate a flow of timely, relevant and reliable information from within and outside the organisation;
- help ensure compliance with applicable laws and regulations, and also with internal policies with respect to the conduct of business.

Effective financial controls, including the maintenance of proper accounting records, are an important element of internal control. They help ensure that the company is not unnecessarily exposed to avoidable financial risks and that financial information used within the business and for publication is reliable.

A sound system of internal control reduces, but cannot eliminate, the possibility of poor judgement in decision-making; human error, control processes being deliberately circumvented by employees and others, management overriding controls and the occurrence of unforeseeable circumstances.

Reviewing the effectiveness of internal control is an essential part of the board's responsibilities. Management is accountable to the board for monitoring the system of internal control and for providing assurance to the board that it has done so.

Reports from the management to the board should, in relation to the areas covered by them, provide a balanced assessment of the significant risks and the effectiveness of the system of controlling and managing those risks. Any significant control failings or weaknesses identified should be discussed in the reports, including the impact that they have had, or may have, on the company and the actions being taken to rectify them. It is essential that there be openness of communication by management with the board relating to risk and control.

Financial measures

The balance sheet, profit and loss account and cash flow statement are the most important financial statements produced by a company. While each is important in its own right, they are meant to be analysed together.

Profit and loss account/income statement

A profit and loss account or income statement is a summary of business transactions for a given period – usually a fiscal quarter or year. By deducting total expenditure from total income, it shows on the 'bottom line' whether your business made a profit or loss at the end of that period.

It begins with an entry for revenue and subtracts from revenue the costs of running the business, including cost of goods sold, operating expenses, depreciation and amortisation of various assets and taxes. The bottom line is net income.

Profit isn't the same as the cash in the bank account, because there are likely to be non-cash items in the profit and loss account. For example, your business might not have been paid for all of its sales. The sales figure in the profit and loss account is for the sales invoiced during that period. Money received from customers in respect of invoices goes on to the balance sheet.

You might come across the terms PBIDT, which stands for profit before interest, depreciation and tax, and EBITDA – earnings before interest, tax, depreciation and amortisation.

Directors should note that the company may only pay dividends to its shareholders up to the limit of the profit after tax, plus any profit from previous years that it has in reserve. The director must check the profit and loss account to make sure the company has sufficient profit available before declaring a dividend.

Balance sheet

A financial statement summarises a company's assets, liabilities and shareholders' equity at a specific point in time. The balance sheet must follow the following formula:

Assets = Liabilities + Shareholders' Equity

Accounts such as cash, inventory and property are on the asset side of the balance sheet, while on the liability side there are accounts such as accounts payable or long-term debt. The exact accounts on a balance sheet will differ by company and by industry, as there is no one set template that accurately accommodates for the differences between different types of businesses.

Assets are things that the company owns. They are the resources of the company that have been acquired through transactions, and have future economic value that can be measured. Assets also include costs paid in advance that have not yet expired, such as prepaid advertising, prepaid insurance, prepaid legal fees, and prepaid rent.

Liabilities are obligations of the company; they are amounts owed to creditors for a past transaction and they usually have the word "payable" in their account title. Along with owner's equity, liabilities can be thought of as a **source** of the company's assets. They can also be thought of as a claim against a company's assets. Liabilities also include amounts received in advance for future services.

Capital and reserves are in effect liabilities, because the firm owes this money to the owners. What a firm owns, it owes.

Cash flow statement

Cash is essential for running a business and directors should pay particular attention to the current cash position and forecast flows.

The cash flow statement reports the cash generated and used during the time interval specified in its heading.

Because the income statement is prepared under the accrual basis of accounting, the revenues reported may not have been collected and the expenses reported might not have been paid.

The cash flow statement identifies the cash that is flowing in and out of the company. It allows investors to understand how a company's operations are running, where its money is coming from, and how it is being spent.

If a company is consistently generating more cash than it is using, the company will be able to increase its dividend, buy back some of its stock, reduce debt, or acquire another company.

Cash flow is determined by looking at three components by which cash enters and leaves a company: core operations, investing and financing:

- Operating activities constitute the revenue-generating activities of a business. Examples of operating activities are cash received and disbursed for product sales, royalties, commissions, fines, lawsuits, supplier and lender invoices, and payroll.
- Investing activities constitute payments made to acquire long-term assets, as well as cash received from their sale. Examples of investing activities are the purchase of fixed

assets and the purchase or sale of securities issued by other entities.

- Financing activities constitute activities that will alter the equity or borrowings of a business. Examples are the sale of company shares, the repurchase of shares, and dividend payments.

Many groups of people are interested in the published accounts of a company. The information they provide may influence future decisions. For example, lenders will be looking at the solvency of a business. Rivals are interested in monitoring the profits earned by competitors.

Liquidity

Liquidity is a measure of an organisation's ability to pay its debts as they fall due.

The 'current ratio' is the simplest measure and is calculated by dividing the total current assets by the total current liabilities. The higher the ratio, the better the company's liquidity position. A value of over 100% is normal in a non-banking corporation.

However, some current assets are more difficult to sell at full value in a hurry. The 'quick ratio' measures a company's ability to meet its short-term obligations with its most liquid assets.

The quick ratio is calculated as follows:

$$\frac{\text{(cash and equivalents + marketable securities + accounts receivable)}}{\text{current liabilities}}$$

Managing risk

Successful business involves taking risks. The purpose of internal control is to help manage and control risk appropriately, rather than to eliminate all risks, since profits are in part the reward for successful risk taking in business.

All members of the board should have a feeling for the main business risks. Furthermore, the board should establish ways of monitoring the development of these risks and seek reassurance that such risks are being managed in an appropriate manner by the management team.

In larger companies, risk management may become a particular focus of a boardroom audit committee or an internal audit department. However, even when many aspects of risk management are delegated to specific individuals or corporate bodies, it is important that the board as a whole retain ownership of risk supervision.

Risk assessment and control should not be limited to financial risks but should also include other relevant matters. These include external factors that should be exposed in the PEST analysis as well as an increasing range of other factors such as employment litigation, loss of key individuals, succession planning, IT failure/data loss, reputation risk etc.

There are four possible responses to risk: -

- Avoid the risk. Do not commit to planned action and abandon the proposed project.
- Mitigate the risk. Invest in standby equipment, duplicate or triplicate critical components, train staff or adopt risk policies such as requiring senior executives to travel in different vehicles.
- Transfer the risk. Insure against the risk or otherwise spread the exposure to third parties.
- Retain the risk. In this case the board must evaluate the impact of a worst case scenario and the ability of the organisation to recover. Different organisations have different appetites for risk, as well as varying resilience to disaster.

In determining its policies with regard to internal control, and thereby assessing what constitutes a sound system of internal control in the particular circumstances of the company, the board's deliberations should include consideration of the following factors:

- The nature and extent of the risks facing the organisation, which risks are acceptable and to what extent?
- The likelihood of the risks materialising?
- The organisation's ability to reduce the incidence and impact on the business of risks that do materialise?
- The cost of operating particular controls relative to the benefits of managing the associated risks?

Risk register

The CEO should always consider him/herself as the *de facto* chief risk officer, and seek to encourage an appropriate sense of risk consciousness at all levels of the company.

Business risk is classified into different six main types:

- **Strategic Risk:** risks associated with the operations of that particular industry. These kind of risks arise from
    - **Business Environment:** buyers and sellers interacting to buy and sell goods and services,

changes in supply and demand, competitive structures and introduction of new technologies.

  - **Transaction:** assets relocation of mergers and acquisitions, spin-offs, alliances and joint ventures.
  - **Investor Relations:** strategy for communicating with individuals who have invested in the business.

- **Financial Risk:** risks associated with the financial structure and transactions of the particular industry.
- **Operational Risk:** risks associated with the operational and administrative procedures of the particular industry.
- **Compliance Risk:** risks associated with the need to comply with the rules and regulations of the government.
- **Reputational risk:** risks relating to external perceptions, including social media and corporate response to accidents, disasters and product failures.
- **Other risks:** risks like natural disasters, such as flooding, and others that depend upon the nature and scale of the industry.

It is useful for companies to adopt a risk register, which is reviewed by the board on a regular basis. This should contain the following categories of information:

- A description of the main risks facing the company
- The impact should a risk actually occur
- The probability of its occurrence
- A summary of the planned response should the event occur
- A summary of risk mitigation actions that can be taken in advance to reduce the probability and/or impact of the event.

Rewards and sanctions for management

Practical aspects of performance management are important because they relate closely to motivation. It is a truism that "What gets measured gets done". However, there is another consideration. Rewards that involve cost are a call on shareholders' assets.

The whole subject of bonuses, in particular, can be a hot potato in the media and at shareholders' meetings. Furthermore, bonus schemes rapidly become out of date as the context and objectives change.

There are three broad types of incentive: financial (e.g. bonuses or penalties); operational (e.g. training/development, or granting more or less responsibility); and reputational (e.g. status or public acclaim/criticism).

When setting up incentive systems, it is worth assessing the motivations of the key players, including the balance between financial and other motivations, and whether they operate at organisational, team or individual level. Check that they only relate to outcomes over which the players have control or significant influence and link the incentives to performance measures that lead to the desired (long-term) outcomes in a predictable way. A single measure might not capture the relevant aspects of performance, but any set of measures must be kept manageable.

It is important to ensure the rewards and sanctions are cost-effective. Where they involve financial elements, it may be sensible to model the operation of the system to help define appropriate values or ranges. Safeguards should be introduced to prevent unintended behaviours, with independent assessment of performance and validation of key performance measures.

The programme's overall performance management cycle should include regular internal and external reviews of the effectiveness of sanctions and reward mechanisms.

Check out your behaviour now

Check out your behaviour and what you have learned against the corporate governance checklists in Chapter 16.

Find out more about director development and corporate governance at: www.corporatedirector.co.uk

13. Strategic Thinking

Strategies and plans

The primary task for all boards is to establish corporate direction. Profit is also the area in which boards find it most difficult to spend sufficient time and about which directors most frequently report the inadequacy of their knowledge.

Consider these results from a Harvard Business School survey: -

- 90% of companies fail to execute strategy
- 85% of executives spend less than one hour a month discussing strategy
- 60% of companies do not link budgets to strategy
- Only 25% of managers have incentives linked to strategy
- Less than 5% of the workforce understand the strategy

The board and the company should develop and continually refine a long term strategy that can be clearly articulated and justified. While the process of developing strategy requires management and the board to consider a wide range of stakeholders whose response to the strategy may be critical to the organisation's success and to give particular attention to the owners, boards should always remember that their primary responsibility is to the organisation.

Although the board exists to monitor management, the interests of the company are best served when directors and management can work together as business partners to promote the business, operations and strategy of the company. So long as the independent directors are able to maintain their independent judgement this relationship enables directors to have a meaningful input into the key business decisions of the company and the ability of management to draw on the expertise, judgement, experience and knowledge of the company's directors.

There should be an annual strategy review – or more frequently if warranted by business and other developments. Directors can help management by bringing to bear their external experience and expertise, and focusing on the business from a shareholder point of view. The exercise will allow the board and the management to make conscious decisions about the best direction of the company, and be able to explain why they have made the decisions that they have made.

Relationships, creativity and focus will be enhanced if such strategic planning can be done off-site at a residential retreat.

Having considered corporate and financial strategic options for the organisation, the board is then able to decide the direction for the organisation. Next is to ensure that business strategies and plans are developed to implement the corporate strategy.

These are likely to be the responsibility of the management – the people who have to deliver the results.

The role of the board is to approve the development process and to ensure that the strategies and plans are consistent with the corporate strategy.

This might be integrated with the organisation's budgetary process and is likely to be iterative – depending on the extent to which the board needs to be involved.

Key considerations are: -

- Plans are consistent with corporate strategy
- Plans are compatible across different business units
- Individual and combined plans are achievable within the resources available, and the forecast revenues and costs
- Plans are consistent with and potentially responsive to changes in market, economy and regulatory environments
- Plans are consistent with legal and ethical requirements
- Plans are supported by the management

Vision, mission and values

A vision, mission and values statement is a collection of words, created collaboratively, that summarises what an organisation is intended to look like.

Its purpose is to provide focus and serve as a reminder of where the organisation is going. It helps to determine strategy and policy, and how the organisation operates, and helps to keep the focus on the strengths of the company.

It should include references to the various stakeholders in the business and, sometimes, broader societal interests.

A successful vision, mission and values statement accomplishes six goals:

- gives a sense of the future
- guides decision making and strategy
- creates a shared purpose
- provides guidelines that determine behaviour
- inspires emotion
- connects to values

A key foundation for any strategy is an understanding of what the company is for and its long term vision.

Vision, mission and values statements have had a bad press, because they have often been developed with the help of outside consultants – and then ignored.

The key is to discover and describe the essence of the organisation – as it is or as you wish it to be – to make sure that it is properly interpreted and understood and then to introduce processes that ensure consistent application.

Developed sensitively and used properly, vision, mission and values statements can form the structure and context for major decision-making and communication with employees, shareholders and other stakeholders.

Vision

Vision means the desired future of the organisation; how it wants people to describe the entity when it has achieved its mission.

A vision is a picture of the future created in the imagination, and communicated in a way that motivates others to act.

A vision helps unite people towards a purpose. Creating and living a vision is the role of leaders in organisations. They have to espouse it and help others to believe it. Most important, a vision should inspire people to want to work for you or do business with you.

Brefi Group's vision is:

> *"A world of work that enables individuals and teams to achieve their potential in a congruent and ethical manner."*

Mission

A mission is the overall purpose of an organisation: what you do, who you do it for, and how and why you do it. It sets boundaries on the organisation's current activities.

A mission statement is a description of the organisation's key purposes. It is a unifying statement of what an organisation is in business to do. It is a key reference point in the planning and implementation of change.

- How you are unique from everyone else out there; your unique selling proposition
- What problem(s) you solve, what need(s) you fulfil
- What you sell; how you make your money
- Who you will sell to; your target market
- What are your economic/financial goals
- What are your social/community goals

Brefi Group's mission statement is:

"Brefi Group helps individuals and teams in organisations discover and achieve their potential so that they can become more effective with less stress."

Values

Values are the beliefs of an organisation, the expression of what it stands for and how it will conduct itself.

Values are the core of an organisation's being, they help to distinguish this organisation from others. They underpin policies, objectives, procedures and strategies because they provide an anchor and a reference point for all things that happen.

Values should be stated explicitly and unambiguously, and be feasible so that they provide guidance and motivation for people's actions in all of the organisation's activities.

To build and maintain the organisation's reputation, boards should look once a year at the way the statement of values applies in practice. Surveys of employees, customers and suppliers can help test the statement of values against the reality of what's going on. Such surveys are best carried out by professional third parties.

There are two categories of value. Generic values of honesty, integrity and trust, *etc.* are essential in any organisation. However, the existence of these values is unlikely to differentiate it from its competitors.

The values that matter in a vision, mission and values exercise are the ones that define the organisation and communicate its particular character. Three to five values would be plenty.

Values cannot be seen or touched. They only exist when interpreted as behaviours. Any values exercise should, therefore, include worked case studies of how each value would be applied in practice.

Here is one of Brefi Group's values:

> *"We are committed to our own personal and professional development. We role model learning and behave as co-learners when working with clients."*

Values are closely related to beliefs, which are statements about what is important and "how things are done round here".

Here is one of Brefi Group's beliefs:

> *"As individuals and organisations are aligned and discover their potential, corporate performance improves."*

Determine the culture

Organisations can have a wide range of cultures. Some see themselves as competitive, with a sporting analogy, some are more military in their approach. Others are creative, or cutting edge. Some are nurturing a new entity or are stewards for a legacy.

Organisation culture is a powerful force and both reflects and shapes the way an organisation operates. It is part of why people work there and even why people do business with it.

You tamper with it at your own risk. However, cultures can become introverted and out of touch with the environment, they can be left behind by developments. Most important, they can damage relationships with stakeholders.

Leadership comes from the top. Board behaviour and director relationships are important factors in setting and communicating a culture.

Robert Dilts' Logical Levels is an excellent model for reviewing the current state of an organisation and identifying changes needed to achieve strategic goals.

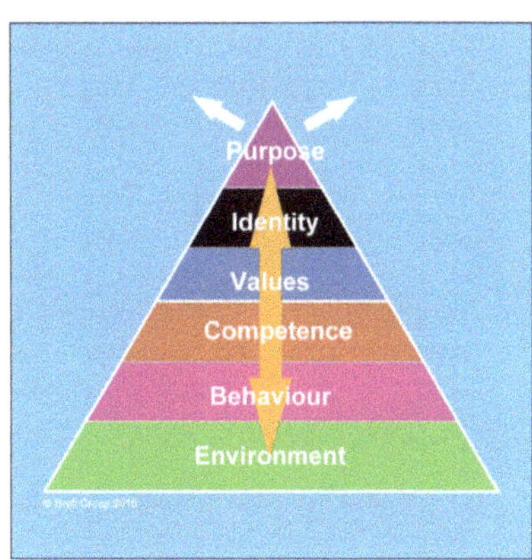

Asking the following questions will help identify the current culture: -

- What is the external environment you operate in – products, geography, regulation *etc.*?
- What is the internal environment of your organisation – physical, social and emotional?
- What do you actually do in your organisation, what are your core processes?
- What are your skills and competences – how do they relate to your core processes and differentiate you from others?
- What are the beliefs and values of the organisation – both those formally expressed and those demonstrated by behaviours?
- What is your organisation's identity – is it cutting edge, reliable, agile, technical, social; is it a sporting, military, family or bureaucratic analogy; is it transformational *etc.*?
- Finally, what is your organisation for – how does it contribute to society, what about it inspires your staff and customers?

When you have the answers, then check – is this what you really want; how could it be better; what else could you aspire to?

- Are the answers at each level fully congruent with the others?
- Are they sufficiently challenging, yet realistic and likely to encourage the intended level of innovation and risk taking?

You can then introduce changes that will move the organisation towards your ideal. This formal culture will provide a firm base onto which to build goals and strategy.

If you take the trouble to address these issues and communicate them to every employee, customer and supplier, you will have a powerful tool that will affect every hiring, every decision, both management and strategic, and every communication.

Market analysis

An organisation should strive to identify and focus its resources on those business arenas where the potential market opportunity exists for it to achieve its stated goals and objectives and it has the internal resources to pursue and capture the opportunity.

Making such business arena choices is one of the most demanding activities in the process of formulating or evaluating an organisation's strategy.

Porter's Five Forces

Michael Porter has provided a framework that models an industry as being influenced by five forces. The strategic business manager seeking to develop an edge over rival firms can use this model to better understand the industry context in which the firm operates.

The Porter's Five Forces tool is a simple but powerful tool for understanding where power lies in a business situation. This is useful, because it helps you understand both the strength of your current competitive position and the strength of a position you're considering moving into.

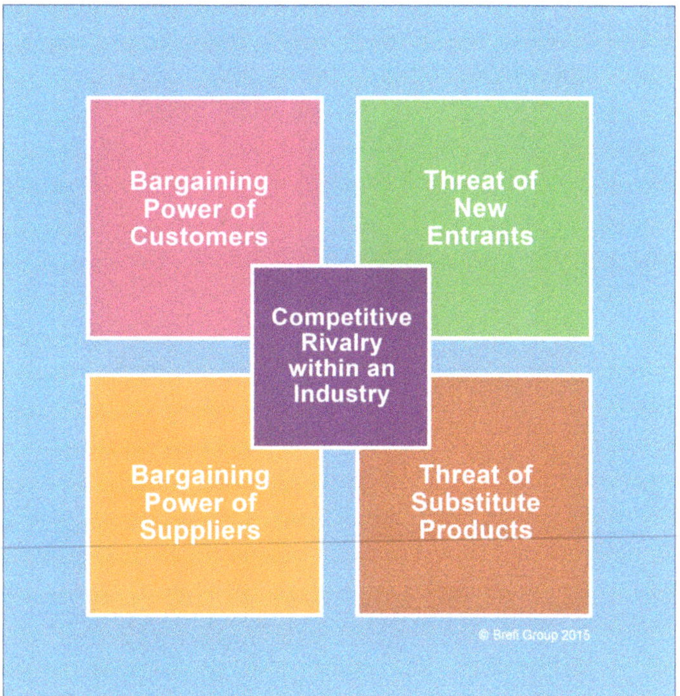

Bargaining power of customers affects how easy it is for buyers to drive prices down.

- Buying power of customers
- Size of each order
- Differences between competitors
- Price sensitivity
- Ability to substitute
- Cost of changing

Bargaining power of suppliers affects how easy it is for suppliers to drive up prices.

- Number of suppliers
- Size of suppliers
- Uniqueness of service
- Your ability to substitute
- Cost of changing

Threat of new entrants is affected by the ability of people to enter your market.

- Time and cost of entry
- Specialist knowledge
- Economies of scale
- Cost advantages
- Technology protection
- Barriers to entry

Threat of substitute products is affected by the ability of your customers to find a different way of doing what you do.

- Substitute performance
- Cost of change

Competitive rivalry within your industry depends on the number and capability of your competitors.

- Number of competitors
- Quality of differences
- Other differences
- Switching costs
- Customer loyalty

With a clear understanding of where power lies, you can take fair advantage of a situation of strength, improve a situation of weakness and avoid taking wrong steps. This makes it an important part of your planning toolkit.

Conventionally, the tool is used to identify whether new products, services or businesses have the potential to be profitable. However it can be very illuminating when used to understand the balance of power in other situations.

The Ansoff Matrix

Igor Ansoff's matrix suggests four alternative marketing strategies which hinge on whether products are new or existing. They also focus on whether a market is new or existing. Within each strategy there is a differing level of risk.

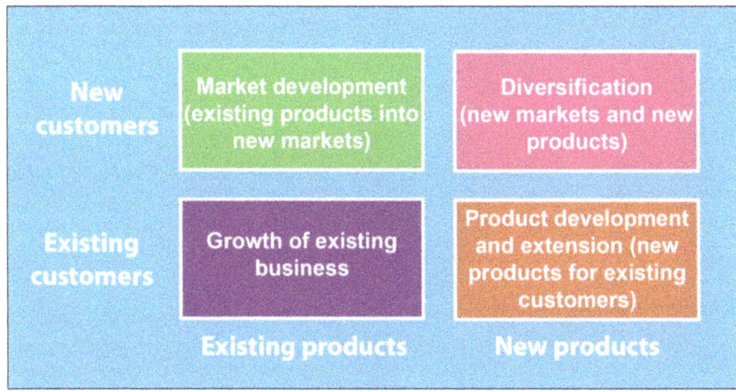

The four strategies are:

1. Market penetration – This involves increasing market share within existing market segments. This can be achieved by selling more products/services to established customers or by finding new customers within existing markets.
2. Product development – This involves developing new products for existing markets. Product development involves thinking about how new products can meet customer needs more closely and outperform the products of competitors.
3. Market development – This strategy entails finding new markets for existing products. Market research and further segmentation of markets helps to identify new groups of customers.
4. Diversification – This involves moving new products into new markets at the same time. It is the most risky strategy. The more an organisation moves away from what it has done in the past the more uncertainties are created. However, if existing activities are threatened, diversification helps to spread risk.

Boston Matrix

The Boston Matrix, developed by the Boston Consulting Group, is a tool for helping companies identify high-growth prospects by categorising the company's products according to growth rate and market share. By optimising positive cash flows in high-potential products, a company can capitalise on market-share growth opportunities.

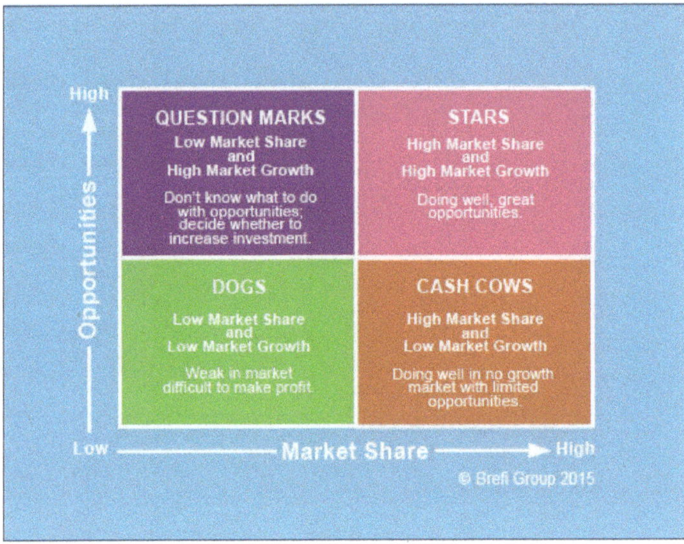

Products are categorised and displayed in the Boston Matrix as follows:

Stars: The business units or products that have the best market share and generate the most cash are considered stars. Monopolies and first-to-market products are frequently termed stars. However, because of their high growth rate, stars also consume large amounts of cash. This generally results in the same amount of money coming in as is going out. Stars can eventually become cash cows if they sustain their success until a time when the market growth rate declines.

Companies are advised to invest in stars.

Cash cows: Cash cows are the leaders in the marketplace and generate more cash than they consume. These are business units or products that have a high market share, but low growth prospects. Cash cows provide the cash required to turn question marks into market leaders, to cover the administrative costs of the company, to fund research and development, to service the corporate debt, and to pay dividends to shareholders.

Companies are advised to invest in cash cows to maintain the current level of productivity, or to "milk" the gains passively.

Dogs: Also known as pets, dogs are units or products that have both a low market share and a low growth rate. They frequently break even, neither earning nor consuming a great deal of cash. Dogs are generally considered cash traps because businesses have money tied up in them, even though they are bringing back basically nothing in return.

These business units are prime candidates for divestiture.

Question marks: These parts of a business have high growth prospects but a low market share. They are consuming a lot of cash but are bringing little in return. In the end, question marks, also known as problem children, lose money. However, since these business units are growing rapidly, they do have the potential to turn into stars.

Companies are advised to invest in question marks if the product has potential for growth, or to sell if it does not.

Beware: All products eventually become either cash cows or dogs. The value of a product is completely dependent upon obtaining a leading share of its market before the growth slows.

Understanding cash flow

To understand the elements of the Boston matrix, companies should be mindful of the sources of cash flow. Founder of the Boston Matrix, Bruce Henderson wrote that four rules are responsible for product cash flow:

- Margins and cash generated are a function of market share. High margins and high market share go together.
- Growth requires cash input to finance added assets. The added cash required to hold share is a function of growth rates.
- High market share must be earned or bought. Buying market share requires an additional increment or investment.
- No product market can grow indefinitely. The payoff from growth must come when the growth slows, or it never will. The payoff is cash that cannot be reinvested in that product.

Blue Ocean Strategy

Blue Ocean Strategy is a potent method for questioning value propositions and business models, and exploring new customer segments.

The aim of Blue Ocean Strategy is not to out-perform the competition in the existing industry, but to create completely new industries through fundamental differentiation, thereby making the competition irrelevant.

Authors W. Chan Kim and Renée Mauborgne argue that tomorrow's leading companies will succeed not by battling competitors, but by creating "blue oceans" of uncontested market space ripe for growth. Such strategic moves – termed "value innovation" – create powerful leaps in value for both the firm and its buyers, rendering rivals obsolete and unleashing new demand.

To achieve value innovation, they proposed a four action framework. These four questions challenge an industry's strategic logic and established business model. When these questions are applied to the Business Model Canvas (*Business Model Generation*, Alexander Ostwalder and Yves Pigneur, Wiley, 2010) the right-hand side represent value creation and the left-hand side represent costs.

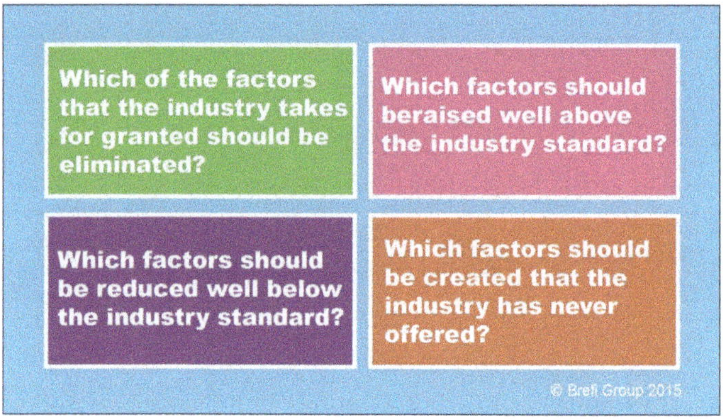

Which of the factors that the industry takes for granted should be eliminated?

Which factors should beraised well above the industry standard?

Which factors should be reduced well below the industry standard?

Which factors should be created that the industry has never offered?

© Brefi Group 2015

Companies have long engaged in head-to-head competition in search of sustained, profitable growth. They have fought for competitive advantage, battled over market share, and struggled for differentiation.

Yet in today's overcrowded industries, competing head-on results in nothing but a bloody "red ocean" of rivals fighting over a shrinking profit pool. While most companies compete within such red oceans, this strategy is increasingly unlikely to create profitable growth in the future.

Red Ocean Strategy	Blue Ocean Strategy
Compete in existing market space	Create uncontested market space
Beat the competition	Make the competition irrelevant
Exploit existing demand	Create and capture new demand
Make the value-cost trade-off	Break the value-cost trade-off
Align the whole system of an organisation's activities with its strategic choice of differentiation or low cost.	Align the whole system of an organisation's activities in pursuit of differentiation and lost cost.

Big Hairy Audacious Goals

The term 'Big Hairy Audacious Goal' (BHAG) was proposed by James Collins and Jerry Porras in their 1994 book entitled *Built to Last: Successful Habits of Visionary Companies*.

A BHAG is a strategic business statement which is created to focus an organisation on a single medium to long term organisation-wide goal which is audacious, likely to be externally questionable, but not internally regarded as impossible. Reason might say "This is unreasonable," but the drive for progress says, "We believe that we can do it nonetheless."

There is an emotional difference between merely having a goal and becoming committed to a huge, daunting challenge – like a big mountain to climb.

A true BHAG is a visionary goal that is strategic and emotionally compelling, serves as unifying focal point of effort, and acts as a clear catalyst for team spirit. It has a clear finish line, so the organisation can know when it has achieved the goal.

Perhaps the most famous BHAG type goal was President Kennedy's challenge to the American nation: "that this nation should commit itself to achieving the goal, before this decade is out, of landing a man on the moon and returning him safely to earth."

A BHAG engages people – it reaches out and grabs them in the gut. It is tangible, energising, highly focused. People 'get it' right away; it takes little or no explanation.

It can be an audacious 10 to 30 year goal to progress towards an envisioned future, or it can be very tactical, such as "achieve 10% revenue growth in the next three months."

The essential point of a BHAG can be captured in such questions as:

- Does it stimulate forward progress?
- Does it create momentum?
- Does it get people going?
- Does it get people's juices flowing?
- Do they find it stimulating, exciting, adventurous?
- Are they willing to throw their creative talents and human energies into it?

  And:

- Does it fit with our core ideology?

Organisations may have more than one BHAG. There may be one over-reaching BHAG and other shorter term BHAGs.

Examples of BHAGs:

- Boeing: Bet the pot on the B-17, 707 and 747.
- Blackpool FC: To reach the English Premier League, completing a meteoric rise through all four English football divisions within 9 years (achieved 22nd May 2010).
- IBM: Commit to a $5 billion gamble on the 360; meet the emerging need of our customers.
- Nokia Siemens Networks: Connecting 5 billion people by 2015.
- Hong Kong Broadband Network: be the largest IP provider in Hong Kong by 2016.
- SolarAid: To eradicate the kerosene lamp from Africa by 2020.

The McKinsey 7-S Framework

As organisations grow in size and complexity, it is not enough to study organisational structure. To be effective it is necessary to coordinate different factors that influence an organisation's ability to changes. The lack of hierarchy among these factors suggests that significant progress in one part of the organisation will be difficult without working on the others.

The McKinsey 7-S model is an organisational analysis tool developed by Robert Waterman and Tom Peters to assess and monitor changes in the internal situation of an organisation. It addresses the critical role of coordination, rather than structure, in organisational effectiveness and can be used in a wide variety of situations where an alignment perspective is useful, for example, to help you:

- Improve the performance of a company.
- Examine the likely effects of future changes within a company.
- Align departments and processes during a merger or acquisition.
- Determine how best to implement a proposed strategy.

The 7-S model involves seven independent factors, which are categorised as either "hard" or "soft" elements:

Hard elements	Soft elements
Strategy	Shared values
Structure	Skills
Systems	Style
	Staff

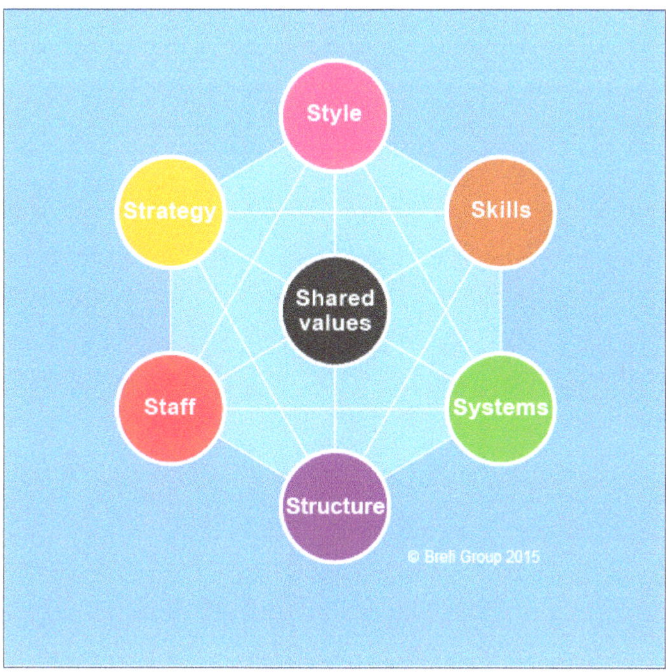

Whenever change is considered, the model can be used to understand how the organizational elements are interrelated, and so ensure that the wider impact of changes made in one area is taken into consideration.

Check out your behaviour now

Check out your behaviour and what you have learned against the corporate governance checklists in Chapter 16.

Find out more about director development and corporate governance at: www.corporatedirector.co.uk

14. Business planning, Risk Analysis and Mitigation

Risk analysis

Regulators are now able to hold boards responsible for fraud, bribery and other forms of corruption at deep level within and even interacting outside the organisation. They are imposing onerous risk coverage requirements on directors that require oversight of internal controls, risk-takers and limitations.

Rapid technology advancement has created opportunity and risk. Cyber security, employees using their own computers and mobile devices, and social media are just three IT risks that are likely to have deficient or non-existent internal controls, which in turn cause privacy breaches, reputational damage and significant investor loss.

Boards should have nominated directors with risk expertise. Every company board should approve a risk appetite framework, including internal control reporting and independent, co-ordinated, assurance over controls mitigating each risk and their interactions. There should be annual third-party reviews, reporting directly to the board and audit and risk committees.

Good boards and regulators are moving towards independent reviews of the board, risks and internal controls, similar to financial audits to provide boards with advance warning on precisely where their vulnerabilities and weaknesses are.

Best practices include confidential and incentivised whistle-blowing and amnesty procedures, and audits of internal controls over culture and reputation.

Scenario planning

Scenario planning is not about predicting the future. It is about *exploring* the future. If you are aware of what *could* happen, you are better able to prepare for what *will* happen.

The purpose of thinking about the future is not to predict it, but to prepare for it. The future is complex; it involves outcomes that are not intended and unexpected, as well as those we plan for.

However, many of the trends that will determine the future are already evident.

By understanding the trends that will drive the future it is possible not only to be better prepared for developments, but to influence the system in order to achieve a better outcome.

Scenario planning is an educational process that helps organisations analyse trends and become more sensitive to signs of change so that they can consider how to respond to events before they happen. It is not about making plans, but is the process whereby management teams change their mental models of the business environment and the world.

Scenario planning exercises involve identifying trends and exploring the implications of projecting them forward - probably as high, medium and low forecasts. These can include political, economic, social and technological. As different trends are chosen and different combinations of forecast levels are combined, a whole spectrum of possibilities can be identified.

The scenario planning process involves identifying three to five possible scenarios involving different combinations of trends and then embellishing them into stories with contexts and characters. This communicates in a more human and emotional manner than a typical business goal and facilitates a deeper level of conversation.

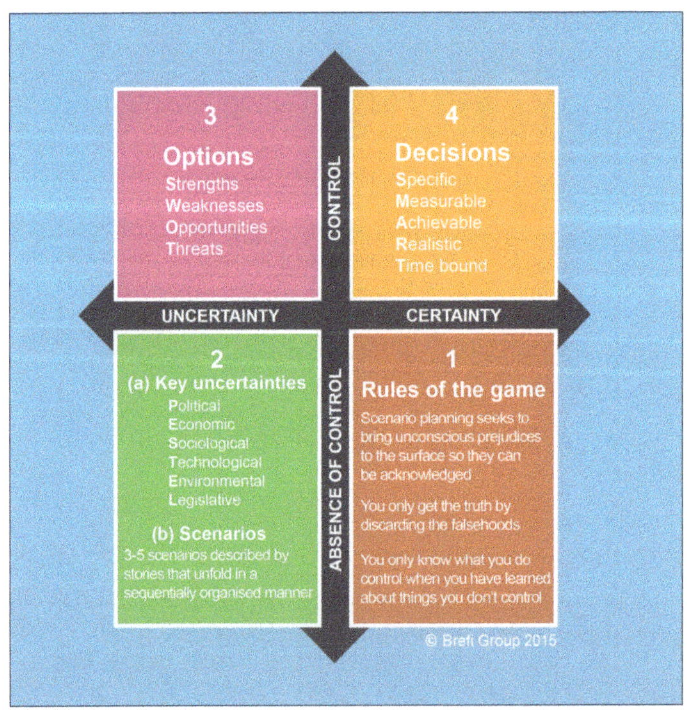

By presenting other ways of seeing the world in this manner, decision scenarios give managers different perceptions of reality, leading to strategic insight beyond their normal experience.

Brefi Group has developed a simple but powerful scenario planning method that integrates standard business planning tools of PEST, SWOT and SMART.

Carrying out regular scenario planning exercises does not necessarily mean that you will be prepared for an eventuality, but it does mean that you are more likely to be aware of the possibility and, thus, able to act more quickly if a situation develops.

Well known examples of game changing events include the end of the Berlin Wall, OPEC oil price rises, the financial crisis following the collapse of Lehman Brothers. There can also be random events (wild cards) like bombs, terrorist attacks and volcanic dust clouds. Ask the great "What if?" question to identify the risk.

PEST Analysis

The PESTLE or PESTER (PEST) analysis is a useful tool for understanding the "big picture" of the environment in which you are operating, and the opportunities and threats that lie within it. It is often used within a strategic SWOT analysis.

External environmental factors are normally outside our control, but can have a major impact on performance. It is important, therefore, that they are monitored and, where possible, forecast and incorporated into strategic planning.

PEST analysis helps ensure that an organisation is able to align its strategy with the powerful forces of change that are affecting the working environment.

PEST analysis helps understand risks associated with market growth or decline, and as such the position, potential and direction for a business or organisation. It is often used as a generic 'orientation' tool, finding out where an organisation or product is in the context of its external environment that will at some point affect its performance.

The environmental factors most often studied are: -

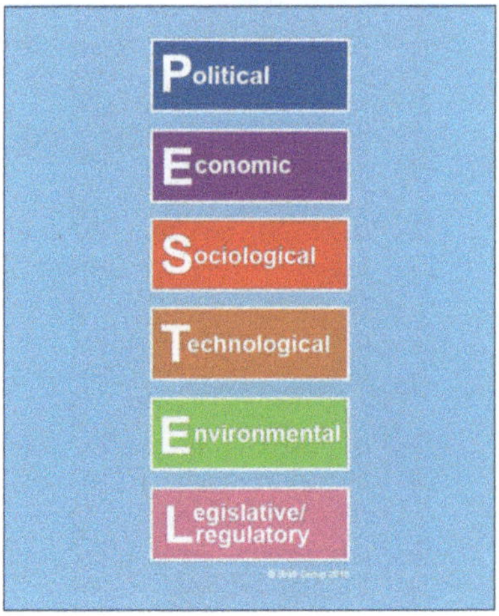

Political
Economic
Sociological
Technological
Environmental
Legislative/
regulatory

Political – Here government regulations and legal factors are assessed in terms of their ability to affect the business environment and trade markets. The main issues addressed in this section include political stability, tax guidelines, trade regulations, tariffs, and employment laws.

Economic – Through this factor, businesses examine the economic issues that are bound to have an impact on the company. This would include factors like inflation, interest rates, economic growth, the unemployment rate and policies, and the business cycle followed in the country.

Sociological – With the sociological factor, a business can analyse the socio-economic environment of its market via elements like customer demographics, cultural limitations, lifestyle attitude, and education. With these, a business can understand how consumer needs are shaped and what brings them to the market for a purchase.

Technological – How technology can either positively or negatively impact the introduction of a product or service into a marketplace is assessed here. These factors include technological advancements, lifecycle of technologies, the role of the Internet, and the spending on technology research by the government.

Environment – The environment can affect you directly and, more likely, through regulations, reputation and best practice. These factors include changes in weather and climate, laws regarding pollution and recycling, waste management and use of green or eco-friendly products and practices.

Legislative and Regulatory – How laws and regulations can impact on business activities and products. Remember that these could apply differently in different geographical regions and states. These factors include discrimination laws, health and safety laws, consumer protection laws, copyright and patent laws. Regulations might include quality and information requirements, and even the right to trade or practice.

SWOT analysis

SWOT analysis is a strategic planning method used to evaluate a project or a business venture. It is particularly helpful in identifying areas for development.

A SWOT analysis must first start with defining a desired end state or objective and then identifying the internal and external factors that are favourable and unfavourable to achieve that objective.

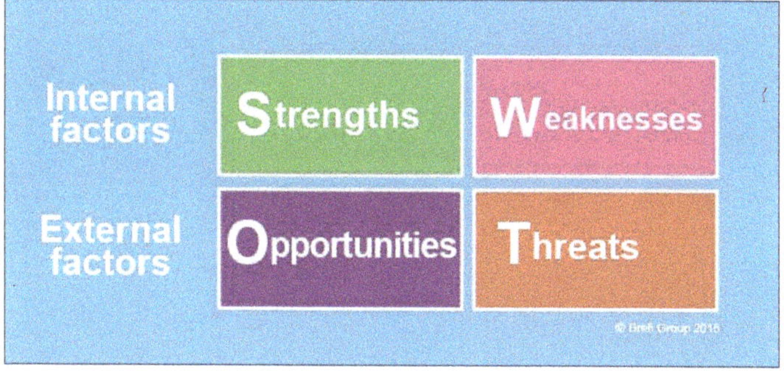

Environmental factors internal to the firm usually can be classified as strengths (S) or weaknesses (W), and those external to the firm can be classified as opportunities (O) or threats (T). SWOT analysis may be used in any decision-making situation when a desired end-state (objective) has been defined.

The SWOT analysis provides information that is helpful in matching an organisation's resources and capabilities to the competitive environment in which it operates. As such, it is instrumental in strategy formulation and selection.

The aim of any SWOT analysis is to identify the key internal and external factors that are important to achieving the objective. These come from within the company's unique value chain. SWOT analysis groups key pieces of information into two main categories:

- Internal factors – The strengths and weaknesses internal to the organisation

- External factors – The opportunities and threats presented by the external environment to the organisation. Use a PEST analysis to help identify external factors

Strengths

A firm's strengths are its resources and capabilities that can be used as a basis for developing a competitive advantage. Examples of such strengths include:

- patents
- strong brand names
- good reputation among customers
- cost advantages from proprietary know-how
- exclusive access to high grade natural resources
- favourable access to distribution networks

Weaknesses

The absence of certain strengths may be viewed as a weakness. For example, each of the following may be considered weaknesses:

- lack of patent protection
- a weak brand name
- poor reputation among customers
- high cost structure
- lack of access to the best natural resources
- lack of access to key distribution channels

In some cases, a weakness may be the flip side of a strength. Take the case in which a firm has a large amount of manufacturing capacity. While this capacity may be considered a strength that competitors do not share, it also may be a considered a weakness if the large investment in manufacturing capacity prevents the firm from reacting quickly to changes in the strategic environment.

Opportunities

The external environmental analysis may reveal certain new opportunities for profit and growth. Some examples of such opportunities include:

- an unfulfilled customer need
- arrival of new technologies
- loosening of regulations

- removal of international trade barriers

Threats

Changes in the external environmental may also present threats to the firm. Some examples of such threats include:

- shifts in consumer tastes away from the firm's products
- emergence of substitute products
- new regulations
- increased trade barriers

Strategies matrix (TOWS)

SWOT analyses can be used to compare options and strategies for desirability, risk and resilience. Or, different strategies can be developed to deal with the four categories: strengths/opportunities, weaknesses/opportunities, strengths/threats and weaknesses/threats.

Often the most rewarding strategies combine Strengths and Opportunities or counter Threats through Strengths.

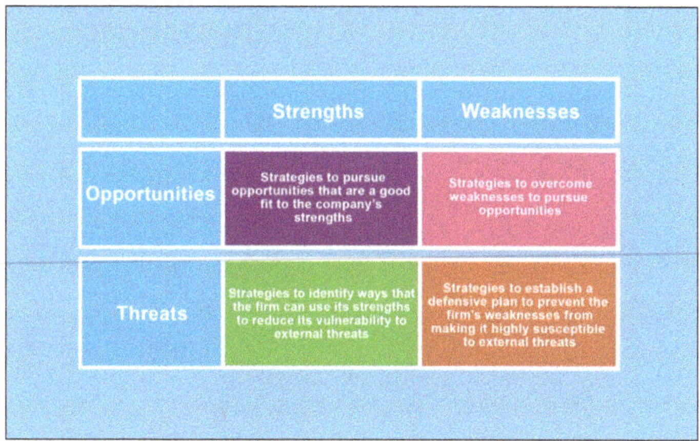

SMART goals

For goals to be effective, they should be able to be agreed, communicated and executed successfully. SMART goals include the components: Specific, Measurable, Achievable, Realistic and Time-bound.

Specific

A specific goal will usually answer the five "W" questions:

- What: What do I want to accomplish?
- Why: Specific reasons, purpose or benefits of accomplishing the goal.
- Who: Who is involved?
- Where: Identify a location.
- Which: Identify requirements and constraints.

Measurable

A measurable goal will usually answer questions such as:

- How much?
- How many?
- How will I know when it is accomplished?

Achievable

An achievable goal will usually answer the question:

- How can the goal be accomplished?

Realistic

This is not a synonym for "easy." Realistic, in this case, means "do-able." It means that the skills needed to do the work are available; that the project fits with the overall strategy and goals of the organisation. A realistic project may push the skills and knowledge of the people working on it but it shouldn't break them.

Goals should also be **relevant** and in alignment with other goals of the individual, team or organisation.

A relevant goal can answer yes to these questions:

- Does this seem worthwhile?
- Is this the right time?
- Does this match our other efforts/needs?
- Are you the right person?

Time-bound

Time must be measurable, attainable and realistic.

If you don't set a time, the commitment is too vague. It tends not to happen because you feel you can start at any time. Without a time limit, there's no urgency to start taking action now.

A time-bound goal will usually answer the questions:

- When?
- What can I do six months from now?
- What can I do six weeks from now?
- What can I do today?

Setting well formed outcomes

Setting well formed outcomes is an iterative process that ensures that when an individual or organisation sets an outcome, or a manager and subordinate agree to delegate a task, they are wholly congruent with the process.

It is based on the psychology that the mind only understands positive instructions; knowing what is not wanted does not give focus or direction.

The logic ensures that the outcome is within the control of the person or group required to achieve it, with the necessary resources and permissions available. If achievement of the original outcome is not within their control then either a modified outcome is agreed or steps are taken to make it achievable.

The questionnaire below checks for motivation and reward, exploring the consequences of achieving it and identifying any negative implications in advance.

Finally, it establishes specific criteria for achievement and ensures that the first step is understood and agreed.

Standard questions for setting a well-formed outcome

Name: Date:

Outcome:

Keep repeating this exercise until you can answer all questions satisfactorily.

1. What do you want? State your outcome specifically. You can define a multiple outcome by using the word AND. Never, ever, use BUT. Check that your outcome is stated in the positive. Then ask what would be a better outcome than this?

2. Is the achievement of this outcome within your control?
   What do you need to achieve it?

3. When and where do you want this?

4. What will the achievement of this outcome do for you?
   How will achieving this outcome benefit you?

5. What might stop you achieving this outcome?
   Why have you not already achieved it?
   What might be the benefits of not achieving it?

6. How will you know when you have achieved this outcome?
   What evidence will you use to let you know that you are achieving this outcome?

7. How will achieving this affect other areas of your life?
   Is this outcome acceptable to you and to other people?

8. What is the first action you must take to achieve this outcome?

Check out your behaviour now

Check out your behaviour and what you have learned against the corporate governance checklists in Chapter 16.

Find out more about director development and corporate governance at: www.corporatedirector.co.uk

15. Effective Communication with Stakeholders

Statutory requirements for information

According to the jurisdiction where they are registered, companies will be required to submit formal information. This is likely to include an annual return, statutory accounts and, for larger companies, an annual report.

An annual return is a snapshot of general information about a company's directors, secretary (where one is appointed), registered office address, shareholders and share capital.

Directors and secretaries are legally responsible for maintaining a company's statutory records and registers; however, full responsibility ultimately falls upon directors, regardless of whether this task was delegated to the company secretary.

Statutory accounts must include:

- a balance sheet, which shows the value of everything the company owns and is owed on the last day of the financial year
- a profit and loss account, which shows the company's sales, running costs and the profit or loss it has made over the financial year
- notes about the accounts
- a directors' report
- a strategic report, which is a separate report approved by the board

Depending on the size of the company, an auditor's report is likely to be required.

A director must sign the balance sheet and their name must be printed on it.

Annual report

The role of the Annual Report continues to evolve. The report has long been the primary source of authoritative information about a company, but it now needs to complement and supplement other information sources, particularly the corporate website. The report also gives companies the opportunity to produce their own authoritative information, particularly important given the significant amount of unverified third-party information available on the Internet.

The Investor Relations Society, which represents professional investors, has defined key objectives and principles for an annual report:

- To educate and inform shareholders (potential as well as current)
- To set out a strategy and report on how that strategy is being implemented
- To report on performance during the period under review and put that performance in the context of the company's strategy and markets
- To explain the risks and factors that could influence the performance of the business
- To provide direction and clarity on corporate governance issues, and to explain how decisions on governance are related to the performance and strategy of the business
- To fulfil other legal and regulatory responsibilities

In addition, many companies see the annual report as an opportunity to build their corporate reputation with a wider group of stakeholders and showcase their company to customers, prospective business partners, staff and their local community.

Key principles for annual reports

The Investor Relations Society further recommends these principles:

Simplicity

The annual report should be written in such a way that someone without specialist industry or financial knowledge can benefit equally from those that have. It should be laid out coherently and organised in such a way that key information is easy to find and understand. As best practice, make sure the key messages are well highlighted and linked closely to the strategy, risks or another element of relevant reporting.

Targeted

The target audience for the annual report includes professional investors (whether they are existing shareholders or not), analysts, retail shareholders, employees and other stakeholders. The use of additional publications can support the effectiveness of the annual report in communicating with these broader stakeholders. However, there should be consistency between the different reports, recognising the cross-over in use of different materials.

Consistency

Shareholders will expect to be able to track progress on key issues over time and make comparisons with the previous year. Unless important to communication, try and ensure the style of writing, vocabulary and definitions are consistent across the document.

Connectivity

Clearly demonstrate the strategic linkages between key reporting contents such as key performance indicators, risk, sustainability and remuneration; this can be achieved both graphically and in the narrative text. Direct linkages between key disclosures not only provides external stakeholders with a holistic view of the business, it also provides internal stakeholders with an understanding of the link between current performance and plans for the future and an insight into how management gains an accurate picture of the extent to which the strategy in place is allowing the company to perform.

Concise

There is a lot to cover in a well prepared annual report and the content should be precise and to the point – quantity does not always equal quality. Clear, concise, well structured text should be used with short sentences, keeping in mind that this is a factual, informative document, rather than marketing collateral. Use cross-referencing if attention needs to be drawn to important points.

Directors' report

The directors of a company must prepare a directors' report for each financial year of the company that lists the names of individuals who were directors of the company at any time during the financial year, and describes the principal activities of the company in the course of the year.

All companies with a Premium Listing of equity shares in the UK are required under the Listing Rules to report on how they have applied the Combined Code in their Annual Report and Accounts. The relevant section of the Code contains broad principles and more specific provisions. Listed companies are required to report on how they have applied the main principles of the Code, and either to confirm that they have complied with the Code's provisions or – where they have not – to provide an explanation.

In general the description of performance and reward should try and explain how the remuneration policy links to and supports the achievement of the Group strategy and individual key performance indicators. The Report should also address increases or decreases in remuneration in respect of underlying performance (including those related to prior years).

As well as contact details for queries on dividends, share transfers, voting etc the report should include a section that provides a history of the share price and dividend performance. A history of the company's capital, including share splits and rights issues and reference values for calculating capital gains tax and indexation should also be provided.

Strategic report

Companies must also prepare a strategic report for each financial year of the company unless they are entitled to the small companies exemption. Directors of parent companies that prepare group accounts must produce a group strategic report.

The purpose of the strategic report is to help shareholders assess how the directors have performed in their duty to promote the success of the company for the benefit of its stakeholders as a whole. It must contain:

- a fair review of the company's business, and
- a description of the principal risks and uncertainties facing the company
- a review of the development and performance of the company's business during the financial year, and the position of the company's business at the end of the year.

If the strategic report information is contained in the directors' report, then the directors' report must specify that it has done so.

External audit

Companies are required to appoint independent external auditors. This is normally done at the Annual General Meeting. The auditors will then report formally whether the accounts given to the members show a true and fair view of the results of the company and the present financial position.

The board should consider the balance between maintaining auditors who get to know the company and the need to change auditors regularly to guarantee independence.

International professional accountancy bodies have laid down accounting and auditing standards to enhance the objectivity of reporting.

Relations with shareholders

Directors' primary duty is to the shareholders – to maximise shareholder value.

However, companies are social organisations participating in a network of communities, other organisations and society as a whole. These are both affected by the company and can affect it.

These other 'stakeholders' include employees, suppliers, subcontractors, agents, distributors and customers. Depending on the size and significance of the organisation its relationships with government and the local community can also be relevant.

The UK Institute of Directors code of professional conduct requires directors to exercise responsibilities to employees, customers, suppliers and other stakeholders, including the wider community.

The UK Companies Act of 2006 enshrines in law the concept of 'enlightened shareholder value', a form of corporate social responsibility that requires directors to take into account in its decisions specified corporate social responsibility factors.

It broadly replaced the old duty to act in the company's best interests, and requires directors to have regard to the longer term and to various corporate social responsibility factors, including the interests of employees, suppliers, consumers and the environment.

These moves should encourage a culture where the wider consequences of decisions are routinely considered.

As a result, directors should ensure that the board identifies and knows the interests, views and expectations of all individuals and groups which the board judges have a legitimate interest in the achievement of company objectives and the way in which these objectives are achieved. They should ensure that communications with such parties are timely, effective and unbiased, subject to the needs of commercial security and regulatory compliance where appropriate.

Directors should also help the board to promote goodwill with stakeholders and be prepared to be accountable for company actions. This should include encouraging the board to set up procedures for managing relationships with stakeholders, particularly at times of crisis (*e.g.* litigation, environmental disasters, takeover bids).

However, it is important to note that consideration of stakeholders' interests is part of a single duty to work for the benefit of shareholders, rather than a separate set of duties in relation to the stakeholders represented in the list of factors.

Directors will be liable only to the company (or its shareholders on behalf of the company) for breach of this duty, and only if the company can demonstrate that it has suffered loss as a result of the breach.

Manage relations with stakeholders

The first stage is to establish processes to ensure that the organisation and the board are able to monitor relations with shareholders and other interested parties.

The second is to ensure that communications with shareholders and other interested parties are effective.

Companies should have some form of formal or informal market and competitive intelligence system by which they collect, collate and interpret information. Directors should ensure that this includes information about their key stakeholders.

The purpose of collecting information about stakeholders is to improve decision-making and to evaluate problems and opportunities to allow early action. It should also be capable of evaluating the cost and benefit of managing or mismanaging such relations.

Since stakeholders are mainly closely involved with the organisation some information can be collected through good personal relations, though it is also desirable to obtain information from independent third parties, including by monitoring the media.

As with all information collection, the board needs to monitor both its effectiveness and its cost-effectiveness.

Communication from the organisation to shareholders and stakeholders can be more formal, with particular emphasis on the content of the annual report and statements to the press and stock market. In some cases this needs to be carefully managed to ensure that some shareholders are not given privileged information; directors should make sure they are familiar with Stock Exchange rules on such matters.

It is in the interest of an organisation to maintain a pro-active and positive public relations strategy. In addition to the specific needs of shareholders and stakeholders, it should promote its vision, mission, values and policies, together with good (and bad) news about new investments, best practice, significant orders, corporate social responsibility, etc.

The chairman and chief executive will play a significant role here, but it is a responsibility of all directors to act as ambassadors for their organisation.

- Shareholders will mainly want to know if the company is making a profit in order to be confident that they can get returns on their investment.
- Customers will wish to know when what they want is available, what the price will be, whether the quality of the good or service meets their expectations and what they can do if it does not.
- Suppliers will wish to know when their supplies are required and where, and in what format, they should be delivered. They may also want to know that their contracts are being honoured and that they will be paid on time.
- Employees will want information on things like what they must do and how they are performing; any changes and how they may be implemented; human resource issues such as contracts, health and safety, grievance and discipline; meetings and actions from these meetings.
- The local community may also wish to know how they will be affected by actions that the organisation and its managers may take.

Although much of this information relates to organisation and management matters and the detail is of no direct interest to the board, the board should ensure that communications, and thus relations with stakeholders, are adequate.

The final piece of the puzzle is to make sure that individual directors and the board promote goodwill and support of shareholders and other relevant interested parties.

All directors are responsible for the relations with outside parties, though responsibilities for liaising with different groups might be delegated to specific directors.

So it is useful to check whether the entire board is committed to enhancing goodwill with these groups.

- What is the formal approach to shareholders and stakeholders, including employees?
- What actually happens?
- What underlying attitudes are revealed by jokes and comments around the boardroom table?

Securing your reputation

We live in a world of increasing transparency and high-velocity communications. Information not only travels faster, it travels everywhere. The rapid convergences of cloud, social, and mobile technologies have created a new generation of empowered information consumers.

In today's interconnected consumer economy, the notion that a company's reputation can be 'managed' as a simple commodity or single dimensional artefact is dangerously outdated. In a fully networked global culture, every morsel of information – no matter how trivial or seemingly innocuous – has the potential to go viral in a heartbeat. Reputations that took decades to build can be destroyed in mere moments.

Reputation strategy is the solution to reputation volatility.

Reputation is a complex set of perceptions, beliefs, and expectations held by all of an organisation's stakeholders. It is the sum of their opinions, based largely on what they see, read, hear, and experience.

Reputation is an outcome of organisational behaviour, values, decisions, and actions. Unlike traditional tangible assets, it is both multidimensional and fluid. Although invisible, reputation can be integrated into business planning and operationally embedded into organisational approaches across business units and geographies to positively affect a company's valuation, sales, employee morale, performance, partnerships, and a host of other critical areas.

A good reputation:

- creates trust in an organisation's products or services
- provides access to policy and decision makers
- attracts and retains the best employees
- drives credibility with outside partners
- serves as a critical success factor for investors.

Before the era of 24/7 media, reputational damage could be managed and mitigated by skilful public relations teams or corporate communications executives. In the rapidly evolving global information landscape, however, stakeholders have greater access to information and can easily uncover actions, behaviours, decisions, or values that are incongruous with communications of the organisation. Today, news travels faster and farther than ever before, and communications professionals need the support of additional capabilities and tools to be effective.

Addressing reputational challenges successfully requires:

- building a system to enable reputation to be used as a strategic advantage with consumers, governments, and employees
- monitoring, evaluating, analysing, and responding appropriately in real time
- predicting where and how communications have an effect on reputation (*e.g.* crisis life cycle, regressive analysis)

- learning how to allocate resources appropriately to gain maximum reputation strategic advantage.

Events happen much more quickly now; news travels much faster. As a result, opinions are formed more quickly, and reputations can be damaged or destroyed within days or hours.

Reputation building is a long-term strategic endeavour. It is an integrated set of ongoing processes, not an individual programme or campaign or one-shot initiative.

Moreover, reputation is not a singular event or state. Reputation has multiple states and forms. It changes over time – sometimes slowly, sometimes with breathtaking speed. Building a reputation that is strong, resilient, and anti-fragile requires top-down leadership, executive sponsorship, and buy-in at all levels of the enterprise. It requires written policies, training, incentives, and discipline. The concept of reputation as a strategy must be woven into the culture of the organisation.

Dealing with surprises/disaster recovery

In a paper published in the New York Stock Exchange *Corporate Governance Guide*, communications guru Richard S Levick says "The essence of crisis management is communication and, in any communications campaign, specific actions – the choice of who is to speak, how the message is worded, and where it is to be delivered – can be as decisive as what the entity says".

It's all about timing, he says. In a crisis situation of any sort, credibility depends on the appearance of disinterestedness. In responding to activists, it may therefore be too late for management to spearhead the crisis communications campaign once the challengers reveal their presence.

The solution involves a delicate balancing act, as scrupulously orchestrated as it is aggressively implemented. As entities match the adversary tweet for tweet – with, again, unstinted transparency – specific best practices for most digital crisis communications include:

- Engage in a way that keeps opinions open. The goal isn't to pre-empt discussion; it's to respectfully lead it.
- Act quickly. Companies can't hope to 'own' the conversation by responding to two-day-old criticisms or questions.
- Respond to adversaries on the same channels they're using – tweets for tweets, Like for Like. The implicit message to shareholders: "We're listening."
- Enlist a social media team. Someone needs to monitor what's happening online. Someone needs to set and

maintain the tone with which management responds. Someone needs to ensure that the company has an online personality that matches its brand and that the company actually takes action by day's end.

The worst thing a company can do as it ponders the social media landscape is to simply say, "This is all too risky. We won't do it." Risk management as a component of crisis management is not about avoiding risk; it is about identifying the benefits that may or may not justify running the anticipated risk. It is also about identifying the risks that *must* be run.

The digital challenge is one salient example of how the crisis communications burden falls heavily on directors who are now obliged to confirm the crisis readiness of the companies they serve, including their levels of social media engagement. It is all the more reason to start planning ahead of need, not just by communicating regularly with major investors but by fostering open dialogue internally as well, to assure a united front once war is declared.

Conclusion

I hope that you have found this handbook useful and will refer back to it in the future.

You can find a wealth of additional information about management and organisation development, director development and corporate governance at www.brefigroup.co.uk.

Brefi Group's Director Development Centre provides consultancy, coaching, facilitation and training for organisations at senior management, director and board level. We also provide independent board performance evaluation and director appraisal as required by the Corporate Governance Code.

Operating at a senior level, your personal and professional development should continue throughout your career. Your next step could be to undertake a personal training needs review and obtain 360° feedback from your colleagues.

Brefi Group provides a free service at: www.buddycoach.co.uk.

In the next chapter you will find a collection of checklists of behaviours against which you can benchmark your own performance.

May your journey continue.

16. Corporate governance checklists

Here is a check list of behaviours based on recommendations by the UK Institute of Directors.

Appointment

On appointment to any directorship there are some essential steps you should take:

- Am I clear about the legal requirements of the role of director?
- Do I understand the duties and liabilities? Have I checked for insurance cover?
- Have I read and understood the memorandum and articles of the company?
- Have I received the necessary documents and introductions for me to carry out personal due diligence?
- Do I know specifically why I was appointed and understand any specific contribution that the chairman expects?

Leadership

Is the company headed by an effective board which is collectively responsible for the long term success of the company?

- Directors' relationships, and behaviour, demonstrate a willingness to be appropriately accountable for company actions?
- Non-executive directors constructively challenge and help develop proposals on strategy?
- There is a clear division of responsibility for the running of the company's business, with no one individual having unfettered powers of responsibility?
- The board has set objectives for continuous improvements in the quality and effectiveness of board performance, including performance in a crisis?

- The board makes available access to external specialists when expertise is not possessed by existing directors or other staff?

Roles and responsibilities

Is the composition and organisation of the board regularly reviewed, including the need for changes in board membership?

- Is each individual's role and responsibilities defined and how these inter-relate between directors?
- Are gaps and overlaps between directors' roles and responsibilities identified, taking account of planned retirements.
- Has a succession plan for directors and company secretary been developed and is it maintained?

Strategies and plans

Are business strategies and plans for different parts of the organisation determined and regularly reviewed by the board?

- Business strategies are consistent with corporate strategy, objectives and plans?
- The board and individual directors receive up to date, accurate and appropriate performance information?
- The board sets targets and reviews performance on a regular basis?
- The board responds appropriately if performance does not meet expectations, or conditions change?

Values

When you have determined the values to be promoted throughout the organisation's operations, taking account of future developments, they should be championed by the board throughout the organisation.

- Are they sufficiently robust to withstand conflicts requiring clarification or resolution?
- Are they sensitive to the various interests of shareholders and other interested parties?
- Are they communicated to shareholders and other interested parties in a way that attract their support?
- Are they pursued throughout the company's operations?
- Are they reviewed regularly to ensure their continued appropriateness, support and effectiveness?

Vision, mission and values

When you have determined your organisation's vision, mission and values, it is essential that the board demonstrates leadership to communicate, endorse and implement them.

- Are they driven by the chairman and managing director, and endorsed by all the other board members?
- What practical activities are taken to communicate them throughout the organisation?
- Are strategies consistent with them and consistent with each other?
- Are strategies and operations monitored and reviewed regularly to ensure long term consistency with the vision, mission and values?

Objectives

Does your board determine the organisation's objectives?

If so, are they: -

- Consistent with vision, mission and values?
- Endorsed by all board members?
- Championed by the board throughout the organisation?
- Clearly stated?
- Realistic and achievable?
- Measurable?
- Communicated effectively throughout the organisation?
- Monitored and reviewed regularly to ensure appropriateness?

Policies

Are your organisation's policies properly supported by the board?

- Are they consistent with the organisation's values?
- Are they clearly worded so that they effectively indicate good behaviour?
- Are they enforced with minimal bureaucracy?
- Are they effectively communicated to relevant shareholders and other parties?
- Are they sufficiently resourced to be effective?
- Are they consistent with the law and custom in all countries of operation?

- Are they monitored and reviewed regularly?

SWOT

Does your board review and evaluate present and future opportunities, threats and risk in the external environment; and current and future strengths, weaknesses and risks relating to the organisation?

- Recognise that past trends may not simply be extrapolated into the future?
- Consciously seek to make objective, unbiased judgements?
- Incorporate input from external specialists when appropriate?
- Evaluate the probabilities or risks of different future outcomes?
- Compare various measures of performance against those of other relevant organisations?

Strategy

Does your board determine corporate and financial strategic options, review and select those to be pursued, and decide the resources, contingency plans and means to support them?

If so, are the strategic options:

- Generated creatively?
- Evaluated systematically in view of the organisation's mission, objectives and values?

Once options are chosen, are they:

- Resourced effectively, taking into account likely risks and financial considerations?
- Supported with realistic contingency plans in the event of failure, or unexpected developments?
- "Owned" by those on the board who have to carry them out?

Structure and culture

Does your board review the organisation's structure and culture?

- Ensure that the board structure and processes are appropriate to deliver the organisation's strategy effectively?

- Ensure that the organisation's structure is appropriate to deliver its strategy effectively?
- Ensure that the culture supports continuous change, enterprise and innovation?
- Invest in technology, training and employee development to support the strategy?
- Challenge the continuation of structures and practices beyond their useful life?

Meetings

Is there a policy for the frequency, purpose, conduct and duration of meetings and, especially, the setting of agendas?

- Are there efficient and timely methods for informing and briefing members prior to meetings?
- Do the meetings enable members to differentiate between management responsibilities and director responsibilities?
- Is there a reasonable balance between time spent on performance review, strategy development and compliance?
- Are minutes focused, accurate and timely, with clearly defined actions and responsibilities?

Performance measures

Does your board have performance measures to monitor implementation of strategy, policies, plans and legal and fiduciary obligations that affect the organisation?

- Measures are complementary to and consistent with management's planning and control systems?
- Clearly identify and explain variances between planned and actual performance?
- Are able to provide early warnings of major risks and notice of changes to the external environment?
- Are presented in time for directors to respond and for the board to ensure corrective actions are taken?
- Are presented in a manner that is convenient, appropriate and accessible to directors – including non-executive directors, who are independent of the day to day operation of the organisation?

Internal controls

Does the board set appropriate policies on internal controls, seek regular assurance that the system is working satisfactorily, and ensure that the system is effective in managing risks?

Does the board consider: -

- The nature and extent of the risks facing the organisation, which risks are acceptable and to what extent?
- The likelihood of the risks materialising?
- The organisation's ability to reduce the incidence and impact on the business of risks that do materialise?
- The cost of operating particular controls relative to the benefits of managing the associated risks?

Committees

Has the board reviewed its committee structure? In particular: -

- Do the board's committees meet best practice, and fulfil the requirements and recommendations of the Corporate Governance Code?
- Do the committees have clear and effective terms of reference?
- Do the committees make good use of the expertise of non-executive directors?
- Do the committees have a proper balance of executive and non-executive membership?
- Are all the committees effective – indeed, are they all necessary?

Delegation

Does the organisation have a clear strategy for delegating authority to management, including reports and measurements that enable the board to monitor performance?

- Powers and responsibilities to be delegated to board committees and to management are specified.
- There is a mutual understanding of powers and responsibilities to be allocated to senior management.
- Measures are complementary to and consistent with management's planning and control systems and undertaken in a manner likely to engender managers' commitment and support?
- Reports and board reviews cover at least profitability, cash flow, investment and risk?
- Focuses on causes and consequences of important variances between planned and actual performance?

- Reports are able to provide early warnings of major risks and notice of changes to the external environment?
- Reports are presented in time for directors to respond and for the board to ensure corrective actions are taken?
- The board monitors management's ability and performance in anticipating, identifying and responding to strategic change?

Performance management

Has the board reviewed its strategy for performance management of senior executives?

- Communicate its conclusions directly or by delegation to members of the management team quickly and effectively?
- Insist that rewards or sanctions are executed promptly?
- Consider what training and development would improve management's effectiveness?

Stakeholder interests

Does the board take into account the legitimate interests of shareholders and other organisations, groups and individuals who have a direct interest in the achievement of company objectives?

- Regularly identifies and reviews shareholders and all key interested parties?
- Knows the interests and expectations of each of these parties?
- Knows the ways shareholders and stakeholders can have influence over the company's objectives, values, policies and activities?
- Ensures compliance with legal and ethical requirements?
- Anticipates the impact of future possible developments on the positions or behaviour of shareholders and other interested parties?

Stakeholder relations

Does the board monitor relations with shareholders and other interested parties and ensure that communications are effective?

- The entire board is committed to enhancing goodwill with shareholders and stakeholders?

- Responsibility for liaising with different groups is clearly delegated to specific directors – and you know which parties you are responsible for?
- There are procedures for managing routine relationships with these groups – and for times of crisis?
- Communications are relevant, consistent, accurate and cost-effective?
- Communications are unbiased with regard to particular parties and in accordance with the needs of commercial security and Stock Exchange compliance requirements, where appropriate?

17. About the Brefi Group

Brefi Group

Brefi Group is a change management development organisation providing an integrated package of strategy consultancy, facilitation, executive coaching and training, designed to improve corporate performance. Its focus is on individual and team development using the most appropriate methods.

It was established by Richard Winfield in 1983, since when the company has developed a rich resource of learning materials, including many that are available on its comprehensive web site at www.brefigroup.co.uk.

Here is a selection of better known organisations that we have worked for.

Brefi Group provides one to one executive coaching, individual workshops and residential integrated programmes. It has delivered management and director development workshops for organisations in the USA, UK and Europe, as well as managing long term corporate management development programmes. Clients have included blue chip companies, smaller companies, public sector and third sector.

Consultants normally work with small, intimate teams but have also organised events for large numbers, varying their approach to suit the size of the group.

Brefi Group specialises in developing and delivering bespoke programmes in-house. This means that delegates get experience that is directly relevant both to their needs and to the context of their work. Learning together also means that there are team building and corporate benefits from a critical mass of managers or directors sharing the same experience and learning the same processes, models and language.

Programmes are interactive and combine behavioural psychology, executive coaching and management consultancy processes.

Brefi Group has two specialist divisions focusing on director development and coach training.

Director Development Centre

Brefi Group founder, Richard Winfield heads a specialist division, The Director Development Centre, which focuses on corporate governance and director development and provides board performance evaluation and director appraisal services.

Brefi Group's proprietary free on-line service, BuddyCoach™, is a 360° feedback system that includes modules for: -

- Personal Effectiveness
- Managing People
- Managing Communications
- Effective Directorship and;
- Corporate Culture

Invisible Coaching®

A coaching approach is a valuable management skill in today's dynamic environment in which a manager's key responsibility is to help others to be more effective.

Brefi Group's proprietary programme, 'Invisible Coaching – the art of natural coaching', is a series of three workshops that can be delivered in–house or by a multimodal on-line programme that addresses the challenge of helping managers to think and act like a natural coach.

Richard Winfield – International Corporate Facilitator

Richard helps directors and boards become more effective by, clarifying goals, improving communication and applying good corporate governance.

His clients call him when they want to bring structure and clarity to their thinking. He can help you identify core issues and make the complex simple, holding the space for you to create your own solutions.

Here are the flags of some countries where Richard has worked.

Richard Winfield is the founder and principal consultant of Brefi Group.

He is a strategy consultant, facilitator and scenario planner who provides transition coaching to directors, boards and partnerships and helps them develop strategy and build teams. His instinctive creativity is in establishing objectives, defining strategies and assessing priorities.

Richard has more than thirty years experience as a management development consultant, including helping the first magistrates' courts service and the first local authority in Wales to earn Investor in People status and a two and a half year management development contract for National Power.

He is highly qualified with a rich and varied career covering start-ups, privatisations and acquisitions with small, large and international organisations, public, private and third sector in the UK, Europe, USA, Middle East, Asia and Africa. A chameleon, he easily absorbs and relates to different cultures, whether they be organisational or geographical.

In the late 1960s Richard gained an honours degree in civil engineering and a master's degree in highways and transportation, followed by a ten year career as a transportation planner during which he designed, developed and commissioned the software for the world's first bus location system and received three awards for developing rural transport policy.

Richard has extensive consulting and training experience in the UK, North America, Europe, South and West Africa, Baltic States,

Arabian Gulf, India and South East Asia. He is co-founder of the Landor Publishing Group and served two terms as a director of Birmingham Forward.

Richard is a Master Practitioner of both NLP and Wealth Dynamics, and has been trained in leadership at the Disney Institute in Florida. He is the creator of 'Invisible Coaching® - the art of natural coaching', is a past governor of the International Association of Coaching and has published five books on coaching.

He now heads the Director Development Centre, focusing on director development and corporate governance internationally as a facilitator and coach.

Find out more at: www.richardwinfield.com

Brefi Group Vision, Mission and Values

Brefi Group

Vision

Brefi Group believes in a world of work that enables individuals and teams to achieve their potential in a congruent and ethical manner.

Mission statement

"Brefi Group helps individuals and teams in organisations discover and achieve their potential so that they can become more effective with less stress."

The Director Development Centre

Vision

Boards of directors providing strategic, moral and ethical leadership to transform the world's economy.

Mission Statement

"The Director Development Centre helps directors and boards become more effective by applying good corporate governance, clarifying goals and improving communication."

The School of Executive Coaching

Vision

A network of executive coach training schools across Asia, Africa and Arabia benchmarked against international standards and qualifications.

Mission Statement

"The School of Executive Coaching designs, delivers and licenses coach training programmes for managers who wish to improve their leadership style and for individuals who wish to qualify as professional coaches."

Brefi Group beliefs and values

Underpinning beliefs: -

- Each and every individual and organisation has the potential to achieve more.
- As individuals and organisations are aligned and discover their potential, corporate performance improves.
- As individuals are aligned and discover their potential, they impact positively on the wider society.

We value: –

- Learning and development. We role model learning and behave as co-learners when working with clients. We are committed to our own personal and professional development.
- The practice and maintenance of high ethical and professional standards.
- The individual's knowledge of their own business and available resources.
- The bottom-line impact of personal and professional development
- The well being and performance of individuals at work, both separately and as members of teams.

18. Index

D

E

Q

R

S

T

U

V

W

Y

www.ingramcontent.com/pod-product-compliance
Lightning Source LLC
Chambersburg PA
CBHW042310210326
41598CB00041B/7339